SLIM for life™

10 Easy Steps
To Permanent Weight Loss
Through Hypnotherapy

by Dr. Tina Heath

Hasmark
PUBLISHING
INTERNATIONAL

ISBN 13: 978-1-77482-165-7
ISBN 10: 1774821656

Published by:

Hasmark Publishing International
https://www.HasmarkPublishing.com

Permission should be addressed in writing to the author:
Dr. Tina Heath, support@slimforlife.co.uk

Cover design, book layout, and editing by Trace Haskins
https://www.TraceHaskins.com

First Edition, 2022

Important Disclaimers

Hypnotherapy should be used in conjunction with, and not as a replacement for, any conventional medical treatment that you may be undergoing. If you suffer with epilepsy, schizophrenia, or if you are in any doubt whether you should use hypnosis, please check with your Physician or Doctor before using this product.

Be sure to follow the Preparation for Hypnotherapy notes. For safety, enjoyment and effectiveness, while listening to the hypnosis audio content, DO NOT listen while driving or operating machinery.

We advise you to go through the material thoroughly and follow each instruction to ensure that you achieve the results you are seeking.

The author has done their best to present accurate and up-to-date information in this book but cannot guarantee that the information is correct or will suit your particular situation. Further, the publisher has used its best efforts in preparing this book, and the information provided herein is provided "as is."

We can't guarantee any results from the use of our programs or any of the information contained in this book, though we genuinely believe that this information will help you reach your goals. Like with any program, your results are limited by your willingness to take action as well as factors outside of your control and our control. By reading this book and enrolling in any programs you hereby understand the potential risks and are fully aware and take responsibility for your own results holding the Author and the Publisher harmless.

For more disclaimers that may apply, please view the most up to date information on: https://www.SlimforLife.co.uk

Table of Contents

Sian Lloyd

Hi

Well I am totally amazed! I am taking the plan slowly so my subconscious has time to let the advice sink in.

Yesterday after a pretty stressful day- I was able to walk past the confectionery aisle and say no to myself.

I am losing inches- some weight- but as it's taken me 40+ years to get to my current size- I am taking the route of the tortoise- slowly and one step at a time.

I am a recovering chocoholic and my name is Sian💚💚💚 I absolutely love your programme- you are retraining me so well.

Thank you so much x it is so much appreciated after so many negative years of subconsciously sabotaging many mainstream diets as I have been unable a accept success at very personal level.

At Slim for Life I am the one in control not the calories or of other people or their opinions. I cannot say enough praise for the program. I am still human, but instead of eating everything delicious and calorific, I will only buy one treat instead of buying the whole store. 💚💚💚💚

You, Tina Heath and 6 others

7 Comments

Introduction

Welcome. Congratulations on the decision you've taken to be Slim for Life!

As you read through this guide...

As you watch the videos
(if you're in the full program)...

As you listen to the audio content
(if you're in the full program...)

And as you take part in the Q&A sessions
(if you're in the group on Facebook)...

I'd like you to imagine that I'm your personal therapist, and I'm speaking directly to you. Pay attention, absorb my words, relax and simply let your subconscious mind work for you in the best way it can. As you do this, you'll find that the process really is life-changing!

And have fun with this - what could be more fun than having more fun? It really is ALL about you!

You have before you an exciting new program - the culmination of nearly three decades of studying and working with human behaviour. Most importantly, this program is the result of the many years of experience in helping clients to successfully release excess weight to achieve a slim, healthy body for life.

Let me say at the outset, that you're in for a treat – a complete mind and body makeover that will change the way you think about yourself, and the way you think about food for life.

Slim for Life is not another diet and no calorie counting is involved. Instead, the program offers a lifestyle change, designed to help you to develop the habits of naturally slim people - those seemingly lucky people who can eat whatever they want, when they want, yet never put on weight.

Though have you ever noticed how they generally eat smaller portions of healthy, nutritious food? They can say "no thank you" to sides and seconds, rarely adding extra portions, and they are entirely comfortable with putting food in the trash.

They waste it in the garbage, rather than on their waist.

This program uncovers and eliminates the reasons you put weight on in the first place. It helps you to crave less of the products which do you harm whatever they may be.

No foods or drinks are taboo, as the program works with your mindset to help you to tune in to what does you good, and away from the harmful stuff.

As you work through the Steps, you'll notice that some things you used to pick at or binge on regularly, no longer satisfy you in the same way. You can still eat what you fancy but find you're consuming it in much smaller portions.

As you work through this interactive guide and listen through the recorded content (in the full program), you'll notice that overeating becomes a thing of the past. Habits from childhood, emotional and comfort eating and thoughts of milky drinks, tea with a cookie, coffee with cake, dinner and dessert, finishing everything on your plate, along with a multitude of other associations around food, no longer have the same draw.

The program helps boost your metabolism, enabling you to burn excess flab faster. And because you're not snacking, picking and grazing as much, you won't be thinking about food anywhere near as much as you used to.

Slim for Life works directly with the subconscious part of your mind. It changes your mindset.

Once you dedicate yourself to your own wellbeing and begin to visualize yourself achieving your goal, your subconscious mind can't tell the difference between what's actually real, and what's in the imagination.

Through the changes this hypnotic program helps you to make, your subconscious will assist you by adjusting your intake and boosting your metabolism, to suit the slimmer version of you that you've decided to become.

In the full program, we've also included the Hypno-Gastric Band, enabling your subconscious mind to accept that due to you now having a vastly smaller stomach, you can only eat tiny portions of healthy, nutritious food.

You will release negative thoughts, feelings and emotions, increase motivation, and feel-good-factor as the program boosts confidence and ultimately enables you to enjoy food more than you ever thought possible without feelings of guilt or worrying what others think...

You are in the driving seat!

> *Success in anything is*
> *95% mindset, 5% strategy.*
> *~ Bob Proctor*

Enjoy your journey to the body you deserve!

It's time for a fresh perspective...

Get out of the rut...

Take control and set new patterns for yourself...

Every day is a new day, a new beginning and a new opportunity to express the new you!

What is Hypnotherapy?

Hypnotherapy is a deeply relaxing process that works directly with the subconscious part of the mind and has the ability to change the way we think about things.

While the conscious part of the mind takes in an average of 7 things at a time, the subconscious part is storing literally thousands of pieces of information (similar to a computer memory).

Scientists say that the subconscious mind has no ability to reject information. It stores everything our senses have experienced and is therefore, responsible for 94-96% of our behaviour, and with only the remaining 4-6% resulting in conscious action, almost all of our behaviour is completely habitual.

Simply put, the behaviour expressed through our body is controlled by our subconscious mind.

In other words, if we do what we've always done, we'll only achieve the same results as we've always got. A clear reason why fads or quick-fix diets generally don't work for very long - you may release some weight for a while, but the majority of people who lose weight through dieting soon re-pile on the pounds.

Our results come from deep-rooted habitual behaviour that we learned in our early years, influenced by our upbringing, environment and mindset conditioning we received from our carers. Therefore, if we want to change the results we're getting, we must make those changes directly with our subconscious part.

Hypnotherapy is a wonderful process that works by accessing the information held within the subconscious, re-framing it and re-filing it, rather like defragging the computer of your mind.

As an example, whilst reading a book our conscious mind might be aware of what the pages are saying to us. However, the subconscious is absorbing information regarding ambient light, temperature, the texture of the pages, background sound, the room, the position in which we are sitting, etc.

It is by accessing these subconscious observations, emotions and memories that hypnotherapy seeks to alter negative thoughts, feelings and behaviours, enabling us to use our experiences in more positive, helpful and constructive ways.

The state of hypnosis itself is a deeply-relaxed state of mind and body in which the therapist is able to communicate directly with the subconscious, in order to find the core of the problem and effect the desired changes.

At no point does the subject lose consciousness, but the state of mind is such that he or she will feel a comfortable, floating feeling, as if on the edge of sleep and will always awake from the hypnotic process refreshed and invigorated, relaxed and alert and easily able to continue with normal daily life.

Typically, you can expect each hypnosis track or session to take 2-3 days to process in the subconscious part of the mind before becoming a permanent part of your behaviour. Each reading and listening will strengthen the previous lessons so that by the end of the 10 Steps, the Slim for Life content will be firmly fixed in your mind.

Releasing excess weight is easier than you think it's going to be. Trust the process. Trust yourself to be ok, to do it, to accept the changes that are ahead and allow the momentum to carry you, so that you can begin to direct your energy with more determination and enthuse more and more about your new healthy slim body.

It's ALL about you...

It's amazing that we can see the great variability of beauty in different flowers, trees, seashells and birds. We should be able to enjoy that same diversity in humans as well...

> *The greatest discovery of my generation is that a human being can alter his life by altering his attitudes of mind.*
> ~ *William James*

Welcome to a fascinating opportunity to learn more about you.

Take a moment now to envision one of Mother Nature's most interesting creatures - a small, furry caterpillar - a veritable eating machine, a cylindrical, plant-digesting animal, slowly crawling its way up the bark of an apple tree just a few feet above the earth.

Secretly, silently, it gorges its way through life, devouring many times its own body weight in plant matter before emerging into one of the most beautiful creatures to grace our planet. Once finding its true, inner beauty it soars high in the air, fluttering its glorious wings in the sunshine, exploring the many beautiful flowers and plants that fill our gardens. It bravely journeys thousands of miles around the world.

To embrace its true beauty, to free those shining wings, to fly high and free, enjoying the fullness of the wonderful delights of nature, the creature must break out of the cocoon of safety and open its heart to its own sacred gifts.

Let this beautiful butterfly represent you.

Find your wings. Embrace your talents.

Explore your own unique gifts and enjoy your own personal journey of self-discovery!

Don't limit your goal to what you think you can achieve – decide to go after the body you want!

About the Program

Slim for Life is a completely revolutionary process that works directly with your mindset and will change your life!

With its series of 10 hypnotherapeutic steps, this program is designed as a 10-week program to lead you to permanent weight-release.

This is not another diet. It's for people who are serious about slimming and are fed up with perpetual dieting, tired of yo-yo-ing.

This is completely different from a diet because you can eat precisely what you want; however, you'll find yourself eating smaller portions of everything.

These wonderfully relaxing, hypnotic meditations will enable your mind and body to recognize that you can easily develop a reduced appetite and lesser eating capacity.

You'll also eliminate cravings, enjoy smaller, healthier meals, and change your relationship with food forever, thereby increasing your self-confidence and personal "feel good factor." It is life-changing!

How does it work?

By accessing your subconscious thoughts and habits around food, and changing them into more helpful ones; for example, eliminating cravings, preventing you from picking, grazing when you're not even hungry, snacking between meals, etc.

We recommend that you follow through to the end as this process is designed to deal with all aspects of weight gain, ensuring that not only do you lose weight, but that it stays off forever.

How often should I listen to the hypnosis mp3s?

For safety, effectiveness and enjoyment please follow the instructions titled "Preparation for Hypnotherapy" before you begin each hypnotic trance in the full program.

To access the mp3s, please upgrade to the full program by visiting **https://www.SlimforLife.co.uk** now.

Important – we recommend you go through the program in the following order:

Bonus #1: Clarity of Thought / Quieting The Mind
Listen once before you begin your Slim for Life course to prepare your mind for the relaxation process that's ahead. After you've completed the Slim for Life program, you can then listen to this meditation again, as often as you wish! The more you listen, the more you'll benefit.

Bonus #2: Release Depression
This one is optional, and is for those who feel depressed (whether or not clinically diagnosed, and whether or not medication has been prescribed). Listen once before you begin your Slim for Life course, and afterwards, as often as you wish.

Slim for Life Steps #1 to #10
Listen to Steps 1 through 10 in numerical order. We recommend listening to each Step daily for one week before moving on to the next Step. Please don't be tempted to rush ahead to any of the Steps that you feel drawn to – it's important to follow each one in order and listen daily for one week before moving on to the next Step. We're creating important changes in your mindset here and your subconscious needs time to process the new ways of thinking. Everyone is different, but in general your mind will require 2-3 days for each audio to take effect. Each session builds on the previous session(s).

Bonus #3: Embrace Your Style
This one can be enjoyed as often as you wish.

Bonus #4: Sleep Well
This one also can be enjoyed as often as you wish.

Know your thoughts are powerful.

Unconventional success calls for an unconventional approach.

Don't be surprised if you feel a little uneasy at times – it's all part of the process...

Before You Start

It's important to define your direction - be definite about the amount of weight you'd like to release.

When you say "I'd like to lose weight" or "I'd like to lose a few pounds" your subconscious doesn't know whether you mean a few ounces, pounds, kilos or stones.

If you're still using the "lose weight" phrase, change it now - we don't want your subconscious to go looking for that lost weight again!

Change the phrase now to "release." You are "releasing excess weight."

Spend a few minutes really thinking about your goal and if you haven't already, write it down now:

Current weight: __________ Target weight: __________

Current size: __________ Target size: __________

Current waist: __________ Target waist: __________

Current hips: __________ Target hips: __________

Goal Card

It's vitally important to know where you're going. What is your target weight? Your target size? Make a decision now. Then fill out your Goal Card.

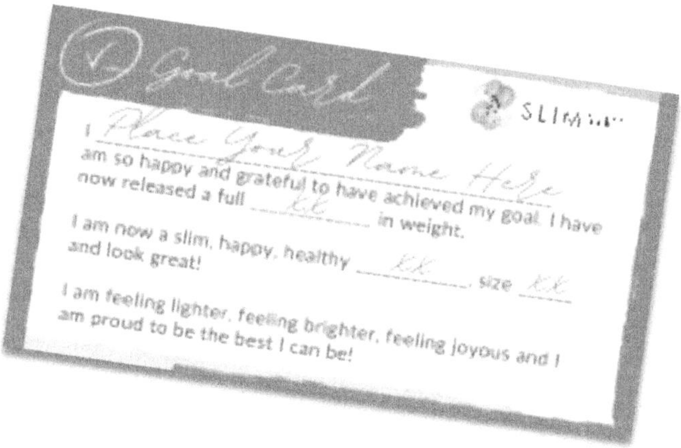

It should be written in the present tense, "I am so happy and grateful now that…" (as if you're already at the finish line).

When you say, "Oh I wish I could lose weight", your subconscious doesn't know how much weight, so be clear.

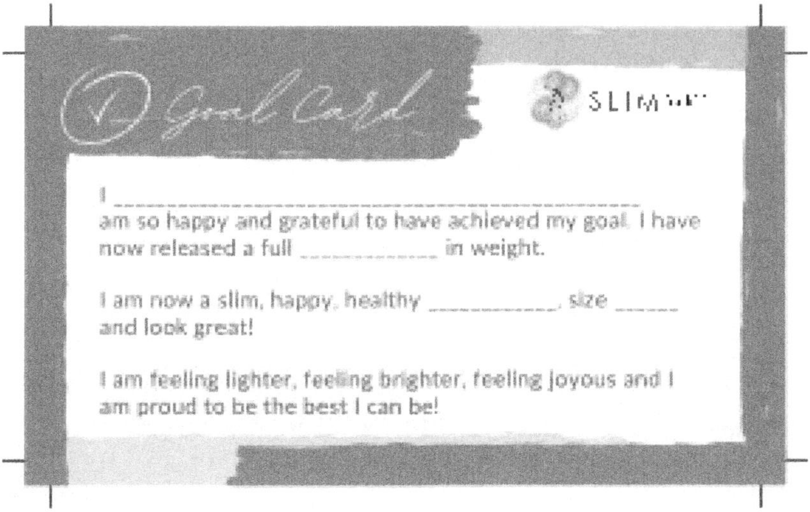

Goal Card

I ____
am so happy and grateful to have achieved my goal. I have now released a full ____________ in weight.

I am now a slim, happy, healthy ___________, size ______ and look great!

I am feeling lighter, feeling brighter, feeling joyous and I am proud to be the best I can be!

Look at that Goal Card every morning when you wake, every night before you go to sleep, and as many times during the day as you can. Keep it beside your bed, in the kitchen, in your handbag, wallet or purse, anywhere that you're likely to see it often.

Practice this regularly. Your subconscious will begin to believe that you're already at your target size, and will assist you by ensuring you eat, drink and exercise (walking is all that's needed) according to your goal...

It works!

We think in pictures. If someone says the word 'feather' you immediately see a real feather, not the word. When writing out your goal you're creating an image in your mind of a slimmer you, at your target weight and size, and that image becomes impregnated into cells in your brain.

Every time you see or touch your Goal Card, a visual message is sent directly into your central nervous system which strikes those cells in the brain that have been impregnated with the image you created when you wrote out the Goal Card - an image of You: slim, fit and healthy!

How we feel about something imagined or real has the same effect. If you write what you want on the card and keep reading it, you are going to start to believe it and it will come true.

Let's Be Honest: Take A Look At How You Got Here...

Take a look at your physical body...

The physical body is a direct manifestation of our thoughts - whether our self-image is one of a positive, attractive, healthy, happy and contented one, or of a flabby, overweight, ugly one, it will show in our physical body. Mental Science has progressed so far over the last 100 years or so that it is possible to locate the core thought patterns that most likely contribute to the results we're getting.

Be honest, where do you store your fat?

Being overweight is not simply due to eating the 'wrong' things. We're looking at and releasing the thought patterns behind your weight gain. ***There's no right or wrong here***, but be honest with yourself please - recognition is the first step to release.

While you read through my suggestions here, try to locate any thought patterns that may be limiting you. As you find them, ask yourself this most important question:

"Am I willing to release this?"

On each point, agree with yourself right now, to "let it go" and as you do this, you'll find the whole releasing weight possibility a whole lot easier - that's a Slim for Life promise!

In a nutshell, holding on to excess weight is the result of fear, over-sensitivity and a feeling of the need for protection.

Perhaps hiding or running away from feelings, insecurity, self-rejection, seeking fulfilment but perhaps feeling it's hopeless, that you're helpless. Maybe you have hidden anger or have been resisting forgiveness?

Specifically... have a look at the Weight Release Library on the next page

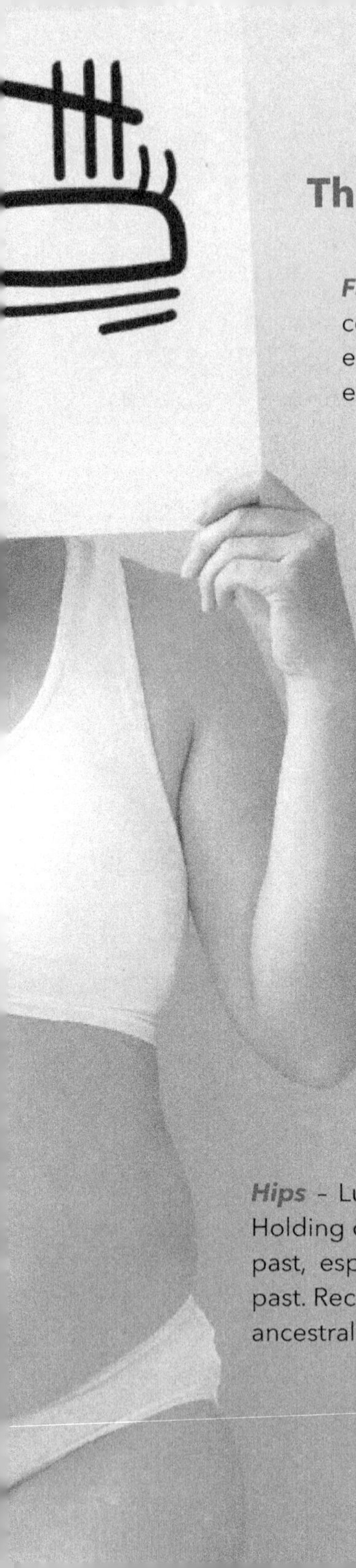

The Weight Release Library

Face – Represents what we show the world. Self-consciousness. Begin telling yourself that self-expression is safe, and, who cares what anyone else thinks?

Arms - Anger at being denied love. Remind yourself that it's safe for you to feel love, to give and receive love. You have all the love you want, because you love yourself.

Belly - Anger at being denied nourishment. Perhaps you experienced poverty as a child, not enough to go around. Allow yourself to nourish yourself with gratitude for food, to feel satisfied and free.

Stomach - Storehouse of emotional turmoil. Be prepared to digest new ideas. Release feelings of dread, anxiety about the new - the new you. Begin to digest life with ease assimilating with joy each new moment of every day. All is well.

Hips - Lumps of stubborn anger toward the parents. Holding on to past hurts. Become willing to forgive the past, especially people who've 'wronged' you in the past. Recognize that it's safe to go beyond parental and ancestral limitations.

Thighs - Packed childhood anger. Often rage at the father or main caregiver. Recognize that they did what they did because it was all they could do with the resources available at the time. Forgive now and free yourself forever, now.

Shoulders - Carrying burdens and representing an inability to carry out experiences in life joyously. We make life a burden by our attitude. Choose now to experience only joyous and loving experiences. Love yourself and release yourself.

Feet - Represent our understanding of ourselves, of life, of others. Perhaps you're stuck in a rut, fearful of the future and of not stepping forward in life. Move forward in life with joy and with ease. Allow clarity, safety and security. Take a chance on yourself and allow spirit to guide you. Release yourself from thoughts, feelings and emotions that bind you to the past. Step into your new future.

Hands - The expression of giving, touching, stroking, soothing, taking, holding, carrying, pushing away, pointing the finger, thumbs up. The hands grasp, hands hold, hands clench. We let things slip through our fingers. Sometimes we hold on too long. We are handy, tight-fisted or open-handed. We give handouts. We can handle ourselves, or we can't seem to handle anything. We give someone a hand, are hand in hand, it's on hand or out of hand, underhanded or over-handed. We have helping hands.

Hands can be gentle or they can be hard, with knotty knuckles from over-thinking, or gnarled with arthritic criticism. Grasping hands come from fear - fear of loss, fear of never having enough, fear that it won't stay unless you hold tightly. Shake your hands freely from the wrists and give yourself a feeling of looseness and openness. Embrace your new future with open hands.

Make a decision to embrace a feeling of perfect inner peace and self-approval as you begin to take responsibility for your life, your health, feelings, emotions, joy and the body you desire, the body you deserve... Slim for Life.

Take an inventory of your current behaviour:

What foods and drinks are you currently consuming knowing that they cause weight gain? Write down as many as you can think of:

____
____
____
____
____
____
____
____

What habits do you currently have that prevent you from releasing excess weight?

____
____
____
____
____
____
____
____

Why do you overeat? Write out your reasons:

Set yourself free from old "diet thinking"!

Don't get too concerned with a step-by-step plan of action. Don't get in your own way.

Create an opportunity to focus on your success through simplicity.

Letting go of past struggles is less demanding of your energy and emotions.

There's no need to force it into existence... just let it occur. Allow yourself to be the best version of you... not the you that other people think you are or want you to be... the real you.

Emotional freedom is everything!

Add Some Conscious Habits to Get You on Track:

- *Begin right away to serve yourself only half portions* of everything to satisfy the 'must eat everything on the plate' thought pattern. If you're still hungry, it's ok to go back for seconds.

- *Drink water.* It's particularly important to drink a tumbler of water first thing in the morning.

- *Only eat when you're hungry.* Stop when you're full. Not sure whether you're hungry? Drink a glass of water.

- *Chew food slowly.* Put the knife and fork down between mouthfuls. The slower you eat the more full you'll feel.

- *Don't weigh yourself too often.* Instead, go by how you feel. Let go of all 'diet' thinking. If you're eating less and moving more, it stands to reason you're releasing excess weight.

- *Quit sweet/sugary fizzy drinks, sodas,* including the low-cal/diet versions which can cause you to seek the missing sugar elsewhere.

- *Alcohol slows metabolism.* Cut down by pouring a half measure and topping-up with ice/soda water.

- *Walk at least 10,000 steps per day.* We recommend using a step counter / pedometer.

- *Don't forget to read your Goal Card - it's vital for success.* Your subconscious mind doesn't know the difference between something imagined or real. The more often you read it, the more quickly your subconscious will 'believe' you're already at your target size and weight, and will help by adjusting your metabolism and eating and drinking habits to that of a slimmer you.

- *Each night as you drift off to sleep say to yourself: "Now that my goal of attaining a permanently slimmer body is fulfilled, how good do I feel?"* Make sure you answer yourself with encouragement. This will help your subconscious to do its best work for you in processing the hypnotic content while you're sleeping.

- *Remember, this is a life-changing process* and not a magic wand - it will take time.

- *If you've never seen yourself in a perfectly slim body,* so find it hard to visualise yourself slim, I recommend cutting out a picture from a magazine and putting a photo of your face on the body.

- *Look in the mirror and smile at yourself.* You are releasing excess weight, you are feeling great, you are achieving your goal - so give yourself a pat on the back!

Quit depriving yourself!

Sheer willpower is not the answer. You don't have to know how you're going to get there, but you need to know where you want to go. It's crucial to have a crystal-clear picture of what you want to accomplish.

> "In the absence of clearly-defined goals, we become strangely loyal to performing daily trivia until we ultimately become enslaved by it."
> ~ Robert Heinlein

WHEN TO EAT

As you go through the program you'll find that many habits and behaviours around eating change.

We can only expect to build and maintain a healthy, slim body when we're eating, drinking, breathing and sleeping in a perfectly healthy manner.

The process of digestion and assimilation is directly supervised by the subconscious mind. When more food is needed by the body, the mind will make the fact known by causing the sensation of hunger.

Whenever food is needed and can be used, there is a sense of hunger signalling that it is time to eat. However, if food is habitually eaten regardless of hunger, the digestive process can become damaged, over-worked, leading to all sorts of other physical health problems including weight gain.

Hunger is the call of the subconscious mind for more material to be used in repairing and renewing the cells of the body, and in maintaining the internal temperature.

The body does most of its growing and repairing work throughout sleep, so it is important to eat a good breakfast.

WHAT TO EAT

It's simple - eat fresh. Fresh is best and in so far as possible stay away from processed, fast food and takeaways.

As you work through the program and begin to trust your own subconscious mind to make appropriate food choices that take you toward your goal, you'll begin to notice that some things you used to like just don't have the same appeal. Your mind will tune in with your body, noticing the foods and drinks that will take you more quickly and easily to your goal.

Amazingly, you'll begin to crave what your body needs.

For example, you may fancy some nice roasted veggies, when previously you wouldn't have given them a second thought.

Suddenly you may crave a glass of orange juice: that's because your body knows it needs some vitamin C, for example.

Clients often report that they can't help but add a bit more colour to their plates, especially the reds, greens and yellows.

In the beginning, you'll want less of the foods that aren't good for you, and as you really get into the program you'll begin to crave everything your body needs for its repair, to re-energize and to heal. Remember, no-one ever became overweight through eating too many fruits and vegetables!

How you feel about everything affects how everything you're interacting with affects you. Your subconscious mind is always guiding you over, under, around and through, whatever it is in order to help you to get to where you want to be.

Think about all your beliefs around food. In some cases it's a surprise if you can find anything you dare to eat. It seems everyone has read something that's wrong with just about everything! But your subconscious mind knows what all those beliefs are and knows how to guide you to achieve a wonderful good feeling - refuelled, replenished, refreshed, healthy, good tasting and the 'wonderful, enjoyable experience' outcome which you are seeking when you eat.

When you go with the flow of goodness that's available to you, you will be inspired to only eat what is best for you. Consider your desires about food often. You want it to fuel you, you want to thrive with it and you want to enjoy it.

Mostly we don't consciously consider what we need from food - good fuel, good taste and good nutrition to achieve good results. There's a great variety to choose from that you could eat to provide all of those things, but instead get fixated on, "Oh I shouldn't eat this or that because..." and it becomes difficult to figure out what to eat.

Fresh vegetables, fruits, nuts, seeds and grains. Fiber found in plant foods is particularly important in the digestion and assimilation of food, and low in calories, but you must learn to trust your "inner voice" - listen to your body and follow its advice.

Through the Slim for Life program you'll learn to trust yourself, to trust your own subconscious mind to understand and guide you away from the produce that may not be the best for you - that's a Slim for Life promise!

You want to live a full, happy and healthy life and food is a big part of the fun of life. Allow yourself to tune into the foods and drinks you fancy - they'll be the ones that provide best for you. It'll become easier and easier as you follow through the ten steps to Slim for Life.

> *I don't eat junk foods and*
> *I don't think junk thoughts.*
> *~ Peace Pilgrim*

HOW TO EAT

Begin with eating half portions of everything! This helps to satisfy the "must eat everything on the plate" habit. If you're still hungry it's ok to go back for more, but you'll soon realise that the half portion is satisfying enough and takes you more quickly to your goal.

One of the biggest hindrances to releasing excess weight is the habit of not eating consciously.

If you've become accustomed to slouching in front of the television to eat your meals, then you're not eating consciously. Your attention is most likely focused on the TV rather than on what's on the plate - you're not even noticing what you're eating and suddenly you've cleared the plate. Perhaps even eating at the speed or mood of the program you're watching.

I recommend sitting at the dining table or away from distractions wherever possible as this focuses attention more easily on what is being eaten, and uses up more energy, so burns calories faster.

Eat slowly, chewing food thoroughly before swallowing, cheerfully enjoying the process, allowing your taste buds to notice what you're eating, and savouring every mouthful. The more thoroughly you chew the better for your digestion.

Select the foods you feel you'll enjoy most and eat in a peaceful state of mind. Focus on gratitude for the healthy nutritious meal in front of you and mentally express full enjoyment with every bite.

Release any habits around gobbling the food down and swallowing it un-chewed as fast as possible - this aids the digestive process and ensures you never gorge yourself.

Listen to your subconscious mind to know when you've eaten enough.

When you feel full, stop eating immediately.

Develop an Attitude of Gratitude - Be thankful!

Your Goal Card encourages you to be thankful that you have already achieved your goal.

Gratitude is a social emotion that helps to improve our psychological and physical wellbeing. Essentially, it's an affirmation of good things. It doesn't mean that life is perfect, but it can help us to appreciate our positive attributes, magnifying positive emotions, encouraging a sense of higher self-worth.

It's worthwhile taking a few minutes each day to think about the things you're grateful for including, perhaps, the things you currently only own in your imagination.

It isn't always an easy exercise, but really try to think about the good things you have, including the good things about you.

Get a notebook and writing down 5 things each day:

Today, I am so happy and thankful for...

1.____
2.____
3.____
4.____
5.____

Today, I am thankful that I am (give yourself some compliments here)...

1.____
2.____
3.____
4.____
5.____

Great – We're ready to begin!

i am
grateful

Preparation for Hypnotherapy

Before listening to each of the Slim for Life audio presentations (available in the full program), please note the following guidance:

1. Do not listen while driving or operating machinery; only listen when you can safely relax, ignoring the outside world.
2. Consider whether you need to go to the bathroom.
3. Prepare a glass of water to drink at the end of your session.
4. Close the window if it's noisy outside.
5. Turn off the phone and any other potential distractions.
6. Tell other members of the household that you don't want to be disturbed for the duration of the recording (30-40 minutes).
7. Remove your shoes.
8. Make yourself warm and comfortable.
9. Rest your head back.
10. Enjoy!

Release those old ideas you've been carrying around about your personal limits. Whether your thoughts and feelings about yourself are good or bad, they will return to you as automatically as an echo... Be sure to send yourself only good, strong, positive thoughts, feelings and emotions. Learn to love yourself...

Let's Begin the Hypnotic Content!

About The "Read-Along Hypnosis" In This Book

Slim for Life is written in 'hypnotic therapeutic' language designed to work directly and powerfully with the subconscious part of the mind to create long-lasting change.

Some excerpts in this book come directly from the audio hypnosis program. You may notice that sometimes I repeat or rhyme certain words or phrases, make statements that are not entirely true, and include some 'metaphoric language'. It's all deliberate and designed to reach directly into your subconscious mind to contradict current thoughts and behaviours to create change and take you closer to your desired outcome.

I specifically metaphor because it adds efficiency. It is simply a figure of speech that describes an object or an action, a habit or behaviour in a way that isn't **literally** true, but helps to explain an idea, or make a comparison to something else that's going on - it's really helpful in getting to the root cause of a problem simply by stating that **one thing** is **another thing**, equating to **two things**, not because they are actually the same, but for the sake of comparison, or symbolism.

So if you think some of my sentences or my pronunciation sound odd at times... now you know the method behind the results ... Because the subconscious has no ability to reject, it simply stores everything it picks up through our 5 senses ... Metaphor and symbolism, rhyming, even rhythmic slang incorporated with hypnosis helps to speed up the process; the language takes effect more quickly as the conscious part of the mind is not fast enough to challenge what the subconscious is absorbing... ultimately creating the changes we're seeking faster.

That's why hypnosis is so effective, and **why** sheer willpower and dieting don't work, or work short term but aren't sustainable.

Bob Proctor, one of my mentors, taught about Mental Science and the intricacies of human behaviour from 1961 until his passing in February of 2022. Bob shared that there are only two ways to change a Paradigm or a Habit:

Method #1: By experiencing an emotional impact (often negative, such as a health scare, though it can sometimes be positive, such as holding your child in your arms for the first time);

Method #2: Constant time-spaced repetition (the studying of information over and over again, causing it to seep from the conscious mind into the sub-conscious mind).

Throughout each of the 10 Steps in this book, and in the full Slim for Life program, we're seeking to create an emotional impact that reconnects **you** with who **you** really are... underneath layers of trauma and/or learned behaviour.

We create an emotional impact that releases you from habitual thinking and behaviours... that allows you to reconnect with the essence of your very soul ... and it's the repetition of the relaxing hypnosis - just around half an hour a day - that works directly with the subconscious part of the mind to create change: long-lasting, life-changing results!

If (or when) you've joined the full program, you'll note that I recommend listening to the audio track for each individual step, one at a time, daily for 7 days before moving on the next step. It's the repetition of the relaxing hypnosis that helps create permanent results ... and one of the wonderful aspects of the audio format, is that you can sit back, relax ... and you don't have to do a thing during each session.

Step #1: Less Desire

Stop eating foods which pile on the pounds. Develop less desire for fattening and unhealthy foods and drinks.

While listening to the hypnosis audio for Step #1 you'll experience a deeply therapeutic hypnotic process that promotes a feeling of whole mind and body relaxation.

Here is an opportunity to embrace the changes that are ahead and become totally focused on releasing excess weight. You've made your decision you've joined the program and it's your time now, your special time to relax and let it happen.

Slim for Life Step #1: Less Desire does exactly what the title says. It helps you to have less desire for foods and drinks that potentially do you harm and more desire for those products that are good for you. When I say "do you harm" I mean those products that you know are counter-productive to releasing excess weight.

You'll recognize that this is not another diet it's a life-style change, and somewhat strangely you'll notice that some of the calorie-laden foods you used to think you enjoyed appear to be tasteless or perhaps you'll begin to notice that certain foods taste old or stale.

The more you listen, the greater the benefit.

You'll develop feelings of calm, inner peace and a greater sense of security. Reduced mind chatter will mean it's easier to focus on your goal - releasing excess weight and allowing yourself to feel absolutely great.

You'll begin to notice that it becomes effortless to no longer enjoy unhealthy, fattening foods and drinks as your taste buds are beginning to change. People often say "it's strange, usually when I give the children a packet of potato chips while watching the TV early evening I used to grab myself 3 packets and munch my way through, but now when I try to eat them all I can taste is salt and grease."

And "oh, that tastes too sweet for me now." You'll be able to comfortably ignore snacks, sweets and much, much more.

Noticing how easy this is, you develop determination to succeed and increased energy levels. The scales may not show any difference yet, but subconsciously you're beginning to embrace the habits of a naturally slim, healthy person - for life!

The cumulative effect of the hypnotic content will help you to sleep better and feel more nourished from sleep as you recognize a very special, gentle connection between your mind and your body that promotes healing.

Confidence begins to take a turn as a sense of pride at taking control feels good to you, forgetting the old you and embracing the new you.

Enjoy the hypnotic audio and remember, for maximum effectiveness, listen daily for 7 days.

Permanent weight release is something you've been keeping from happening.

The biggest part of releasing unwanted weight is believing you can do it, and realizing it's not going to happen overnight.

Give yourself time to enjoy the process.

READ-ALONG HYPNOSIS – STEP #1

The best way to benefit from the Slim for Life™ hypnosis experience is to upgrade to the full online program, which contains the audio tracks.

The following pages contain a version of the tracks converted into a "read-along" format, which will serve as a wonderful preview and jumpstart into what awaits you inside the full program.

~ ~ ~ ~ ~ ~ ~ ~

I recommend sitting comfortably and reading this hypnotic excerpt, imagining that I'm speaking directly with you:

Take a moment to think again about how much weight you intend to release. Think about your target weight, your ideal size and perfect shape. Think about how good you will feel, how good you will look and how proud you can be achieving that slim, healthy body you desire. Get that vision really clear in your mind.

Enjoy the feeling of allowing my words to register deep into the subconscious part of your mind as you become receptive to my suggestions which are entirely for your benefit and wellbeing.

You are of course aware of your desire to eat good food. Your body needs good food to remain healthy, agile and strong. You are also aware of an abundance of foods which are good, healthy and nutritious and, that there are foods which can do you harm, make you fat and make you feel sad, guilty, unworthy or angry, and so on. These negative emotions harm you, also causing stress and causing your body to store fat.

Now that you have made your decision to release all that excess weight and to respect and protect your own body, maybe it's time to allow yourself to feel pleasantly surprised at how easily you will be able to achieve your goal - a slim, healthy, attractive body, for life.

I wonder if you can imagine how many people easily give up on their goals. Some say that they do not have the drive or determination to succeed, to lose weight and make those changes for themselves that they wish to make, and which are absolutely necessary to improve the quality of their life.

That person who has no drive and no determination and no vision is not relaxing here reading these words today. You have all that you need to do all of those things and to achieve your worthwhile goals, but there is just one thing that you do not have yet and that is the self-confidence that you need to believe in your ability to achieve your goals - an inner wisdom, an inner knowing, a feeling of self-trust that you can allow right now because no way is easier than this!

Recognize that you can develop a feeling of confidence, of being committed to your own wellbeing - setting out on your journey completely satisfied that you will complete the trip safely, quickly and easily. Sensing a gentle connection with your perfect inner self that assures you that you can, you will, that you have all the confidence you need to succeed.

However, as you know, nobody likes to be told what to do and if I were able to tell you what to do, then you would have no need at all to be relaxing here now. You'd simply call me on the phone and say: "Hi there, I'd like to lose weight. I want to be Slim for Life. I want to be fit and healthy and happy for the rest of my life. I'd like to be able to wear the clothes I choose in a smaller size and stay that way, permanently Slim for Life!"

And I would say to you "Congratulations! That's a wonderful idea. I'm so proud of you! Stop over-eating and stop eating those foods that are unhealthy and fattening. Instead eat only those foods which are healthy and non-fattening. Do it right now. Stop over-drinking and drinking those drinks that are unhealthy and fattening and instead drink only those drinks which are healthy and non-fattening. Do it right now!"

Nobody likes to be told what to do. So I wouldn't say to you that the habit of over-eating and over-drinking those products that make you fat can be dangerous. They are dangerous and prevent you from having the body that you desire; the body that you are entitled to; the body that you deserve – slim, healthy, and strong - the body you dream of.

I needn't tell you that you will get no pleasure from dairy foods such as butter, cheese, milk, cream and ice cream, or any dairy products that are so high in fat content, high in calories. Fattening and unhealthy foods, you will get no pleasure from over-eating.

I needn't tell you that you will get no joy from bread, potatoes, rice and pasta, or from any carbohydrates that are so high in fat content and high in calories. Fattening and unhealthy foods, you will get no joy from over-eating.

I needn't tell you that you will get no satisfaction from sugar, cakes, cookies or sweets and chocolate and deserts that are so high in fat content, so high in sugar, high in calories. Fattening and unhealthy foods, you will get no satisfaction from over-eating.

I needn't tell you that you will get no pleasure from snacking, picking and grazing on crisps and nibbles, nuts and snacks that are so high in fat content and high in calories. Fattening and unhealthy foods, you will get no pleasure from over-eating.

I needn't tell you that you will get no enjoyment from drinking sweet fizzy drinks, sodas, alcohol and any drinks that are so high in calories. Fattening and unhealthy drinks, you will get no enjoyment from over-drinking.

However, I will tell you that you can become aware of feelings of great pride and accomplishment when you choose foods and drinks that are healthy and non-fattening.

I need never say to you that consuming unhealthy, fattening food and drink is no substitute for lack of adequate stimulation in your life, or for the love that you need and are entitled to. I need never tell you that you do not need to eat or drink more than is necessary to maintain your body at the size and weight you dream of.

Although, one thing I will say to you is, that controlling your eating and drinking is not something that you will not find easy. When you study this program regularly you will no longer be that person who consumes those products which are unhealthy and fattening.

You know, and I know that you know, that you have a desire for sweets and chocolate, cookies, cakes, nuts and crisps, snacks, bread, potatoes and all kinds of unhelpful products. You know, and I know that you know, that you have a desire for creamy dairy choices containing lots of fat, and sweet sugary deserts, and you know you enjoy alcohol and fizzy drinks. You know, and I know that you know, nobody can talk you out of it! However, what I know you also know now, that you didn't know before is, that you also have an enormous amount of LESS DESIRE and you can get to explore this idea of LESS DESIRE as it flows through your body now from the top of your head down through to the tips of your fingers and the tips of your toes, as it expands and reaches deeper and deeper and the feelings of LESS DESIRE can reach even deeper and the time of LESS DESIRE can grow longer and longer, and no way is easier than this.

It's good to finally resolve those feelings and simply let go. Not needing to know how the subconscious mind knows what to do for you - thinking without an awareness of things, thoughts, changing old beliefs, learning new meanings and new ways of doing things without the need to know those things that are done automatically.

You now know what to do and it's entirely up to you. I would prefer that you stop consuming unhealthy, fattening foods right away, immediately. It's entirely up to you to discover the time today, the best time and the best way for you. Some people wait for a whole hour. Some wait until they have used up stocks of food from home. Some stop entirely before bed. You get to choose a time today when you free yourself forever from this unhealthy lifestyle, release yourself from this unhealthy, fattening food and drink habit forever.

We have all suffered the loss of someone we love, or a situation we value and we can be aware that gone is an important part of our life - a chapter has come to an end, it's story told and what now? You can become aware of the responsibility you have toward those who love you and care for you, those who you love and care for - special people who rely on you to be there for them. Embrace the responsibility that is yours and yours alone to ensure that those people will not be faced with the loss of that person whom they love and treasure. Take responsibility to ensure that you live a healthy, happy, long and fulfilling life. Commit now to an attitude of respecting and protecting your body, cherishing your gift of life - that person eating and drinking only what's needed and in the right amounts and at the right times.

You can waste food. You can throw it into the trash, or you can waste food on your waist ... waste or waist, or waste to waist ... Think about that for a moment. I wonder which you will prefer?

From now on, whenever you see those products which are unhealthy and you know will pile on the pounds, your subconscious mind can remind you in a manner that is instant and powerful guiding you and supporting you, reminding you of your commitment to yourself and to your decision to be Slim for Life with images of you that have distressed you, and those feelings of guilt and sadness that attend that fat, sluggish, overweight person that you used to be.

You accept now, without the slightest reservation the total responsibility for your body, your health, comfort, wellbeing, happiness. You are now your own person - proud, confident and in control with that problem finally resolved.

And so before coming back from that place and returning to this place, I'd like you to take a moment to remember every positive thought you've ever had about yourself ... and smile ... How good does that feel?

Step #2: Stop Overeating

Clear the mental blocks which cause weight gain.

Learn to feel satisfied with smaller portions of healthy nutritious food.

Use the power of your mind to slim your body.

While listening to the hypnosis audio for Step #2 you'll experience a deeply therapeutic hypnotic process that helps you to reconnect with the gentle, yet so powerful, connection between your mind and your physical body, and a sense of heightened awareness that promotes inner healing.

This is an opportunity to further embrace the changes that are ahead and become even more focused on letting go of the excess weight you've decided. Again, you get to go inside your mind and turn the world off, allowing your subconscious mind to examine the various ways you can take control of your portion servings.

Slim for Life Step #2: Stop Overeating clears away any mental and emotional blocks that caused the weight gain in the first place, tuning you in to the certain recognition that you have an inbuilt ability to use the power of your subconscious mind to slim your body.

Re-affirming that this is not, yet another yo-yoing diet - it's a life-style change, a mindset change. The growing feelings of calm, inner peace and tranquillity cause more balance, a greater sense of security, reduced mind chatter, less overwhelm and feelings of being in control.

Before perhaps you would have eaten just eat for eating's sake. Now you're beginning to notice when you're hungry and importantly, when you're not, and only eating when you are hungry. Sensing pride and feeling satisfied with smaller portions of healthy nutritious food and becoming quite easily, effortlessly aware that self-sabotaging patterns of behaviour are diminishing as you no longer want to overeat.

You can now give yourself large portions of self-confidence, huge portions of self-esteem, enormous portions of self-belief and massive portions of self-congratulations at simply making the decision for yourself that you deserve better health, happiness, wellbeing. You deserve to be Slim for Life.

Enjoy the hypnotic audio - and remember, for maximum effectiveness, listen daily for 7 days.

> *"The thoughts that we repeatedly think become habitual, and make us what we are."*
> *~ Goethe*

Don't brood over potential problems.

If you continually think you're overweight, you'll stay that way...

Practice seeing yourself as a slim, fit, healthy, agile person...

Enjoying perfect health every day!

READ-ALONG HYPNOSIS – STEP #2

The best way to benefit from the Slim for Life™ hypnosis experience is to upgrade to the full online program, which contains the audio tracks.

The following pages contain a version of the tracks converted into a "read-along" format, which will serve as a wonderful preview and jumpstart into what awaits you inside the full program.

~ ~ ~ ~ ~ ~ ~ ~

I recommend sitting comfortably and reading this hypnotic excerpt slowly, imagining that I'm speaking directly with you:

Take a moment to think again about how much weight you intend to release. Think about your target weight, your ideal size and perfect shape. Think about how good you will feel, how good you will look and how proud you can be achieving that slim, healthy body you deserve. Get that vision really clear in your mind.

Enjoy the feeling of allowing my words to register deep into the subconscious part of your mind as you become receptive to my suggestions which are entirely for your benefit and wellbeing.

Notice your breathing and imagine that you're breathing in peace and harmony and with each outward breath, release all unwanted thoughts, feelings and behaviours as you connect now with the natural life and energy of the Universe.

This is your time, your special time with nobody wanting anything, or expecting anything. It's your time to relax and focus on personal wellbeing. Focus on your goal of releasing all that unwanted weight to feel great in achieving your slim, healthy goal with no need for any more dieting ... you are Slim for Life.

So take a deep breath now and then as you breathe out you can concentrate fully on that thing which is so important – that habit of overeating unhealthy and fattening foods - something that you really do want to change, but you and I both know that there is something stopping you.

I know that changing that overeating habit really is important to you. I would also like you to know that what I have so often found is that there is an unconscious part of you that is preventing you from making those changes that you really do wish to make.

If that is the case here, now I would like to ask that part of you to come forward and make itself known to you in some safe way that you can recognize and understand. So please take a moment to go deep inside now into your own inner mind to wherever you need to go to become aware of that part of you that is responsible for this habit of over-eating and over-drinking fattening and unhealthy produce.

It is difficult for me to know how you will experience that part of you that is responsible for your overeating of fattening and unhealthy foods habit. It may be a familiar experience or one that is completely unique to you. It could be something that you'll see in your mind's eye, perhaps a picture, something you see on TV, a photograph or perhaps it will be a face, or a scene. It could be any visual image or perhaps it may make itself known to you as a voice or a sound and this could be your own voice or that of another person, someone you know, or someone you do not. Perhaps you will experience it as a feeling or an emotion of some kind. There's no right or wrong here. As you now go deep into your own inner mind, I am asking with respect that that part of you that is responsible for this over-indulgence, this over-eating and over-drinking unhealthy and fattening foods habit allows itself to be made known to you in some safe way.

Please take your time here as this is vitally important. Are you experiencing anything that could be that part now, allowing you to be aware of it?

It could be that your subconscious mind may or may not be happy with your experiencing in this way, but please proceed with the understanding that your subconscious mind will understand and will co-operate here today, whether it is happy about it or not.

That's good! And now you can allow that experience to grow and expand so that you can be sure of that communication. I would like to thank that part for coming forward and I suggest that you do too. You can know that the part of you that is responsible for your over-eating and over-drinking fattening and unhealthy foods deserves respect. It is obviously very powerful because even though you have wanted to make this change for quite a long time, you haven't been able to do so. I also understand that this part of you that is responsible for your over-indulgence habit will change only when it is ready to do so. I'd like to suggest to you that in some way, over-eating and perhaps also over-drinking, especially alcohol or fizzy sodas has, in the past, provided some benefits and has been useful to you, in the past. In some way you have gained an advantage.

Okay. I fully understand that the experience of the behaviour of that part responsible for your over-indulgence, over-eating and over-drinking unhealthy and fattening produce has been the cause of negative and unhealthy consequences for you. However, what I am suggesting to you is, that you now re-examine your own personal understanding of the intention of that part and accept that it has been doing this in order to help you and to benefit you in some particular way. Now take some time and go deep into your own inner mind and become fully aware of precisely what the benefits and advantages have been for you.

Perhaps that part has been helping you to avoid something that is unpleasant or painful. Perhaps that part has helped you to achieve something that you desired. Perhaps that part has been helping you in providing a relief or a substitute for something or someone that is missing from your life. Maybe the love that you need and are entitled to or perhaps the self-confidence that you need to succeed and to achieve what you want.

There is perhaps a tendency to associate fat, overweight people with being slow, lazy, boring, unintelligent; and so being overweight could be an excuse for not trying. It is not expected and so the pressure is relieved. Or 'members of the opposite sex will not be able to hurt me if I am unattractive - they will leave me alone.' Your subconscious mind, that part of you will allow you now to know the truth and how it has done what it has done to help you. I am asking you again to assume that the part of you responsible for your over-indulgence has continued up to now because it has helped you or benefited you in some way. Please become aware now while it is comfortable and safe to do so, of just how this over-eating and over-drinking fattening and unhealthy foods habit has helped you in the past.

Now, keeping those benefits or perhaps we can call them bonuses or pay-offs in mind, I would like to suggest to your subconscious mind that there are alternative patterns of behaviour, of experiencing, of perception that can provide for you those benefits and pay-offs provided in the past by over-indulgence, but that can be much healthier, more satisfying for you and allow you to be healthier, happier, to become Slim for Life. Yes ... slim forever.

So now that you have constructed new patterns of behaviour and of perception which are more beneficial and yet still provide you with the benefits which are important to you ... now ... I want you once again to go deep inside your subconscious mind and ask if there is any part of you which objects to these new arrangements that will allow you to eat correctly, to drink correctly the right foods and the right drinks, in the right amounts at the right times to achieve that slim, healthy, happy body that you desire and that you deserve - Slim for Life.

Go ahead now and find out the answer. Are there any objections to these new, alternative patterns of behaviour?

No? ... Okay, that's good. That's very pleasing. You have constructed for yourself new and beneficial patterns of behaviour that will allow your subconscious mind to help you with positive, beneficial habit-forming affirmations to ensure that you achieve all of your worthwhile goals. I suggest that you now thank your subconscious for its co-operation and that you consciously work with it towards your goal - the slim, healthy, happy body that you deserve - Slim for Life.

You accept now, without the slightest reservation, the total responsibility for your body, your health, comfort, wellbeing, and happiness. You are now your own person - proud, confident and in control with that problem finally resolved.

And so before coming back from that place and returning to this place, I'd like you to take a moment to remember every positive thought you've ever had about yourself ... and smile ... How good does that feel?

Step #3: Habit Control

Conquer cravings.

Stop bingeing, snacking, picking and obsessing about foods, especially when you're not even hungry!

While listening to the hypnosis audio for Step #3 you'll begin to become familiar with the deeply therapeutic meditative process that promotes healing. In fact by now your subconscious mind is probably beginning to look forward to, and really enjoy the time spent relaxing, going deep inside your mind and turning the world off while you focus on your own personal wellbeing.

Slim for Life Step #3: Habit Control gives your subconscious mind an opportunity to spend some time seeking out, identifying and eliminating destructive behaviours in your lifestyle and habits around food and drink.

As you listen to the hypnotic content you begin to become aware that you no longer need to think about food unless you are hungry. It really is a life-changing experience.

Feeling calmer and more peaceful, more secure through releasing the mind chatter that used to overwhelm you from time to time, your new-found sense of clarity enables you to find feelings that serve and support, rather than irritate and overwhelm. You no longer allow things to get to you.

Becoming more and more aware that you're releasing old unhelpful, unsupportive habits around food and drink, and replacing them with new habits that are constructive, enjoyable and comfortable - the habits of those of naturally slim people I mentioned in the introduction.

No longer do you feel the urge to binge, eat snacks, graze and pick at the leftovers. No longer are you obsessing about food, especially when you're not even hungry!

New confidence is emerging as you feel more relaxed about eating out in restaurants and bars, for eating, drinking and socializing with friends is such a pleasure. Sleeping better and feeling more nourished from sleep as eating more healthily is naturally improving your overall health. Energy levels are soaring and people are beginning to notice how well you're looking. How good do you feel?

Enjoy the hypnotic audio - and remember, for maximum effectiveness, listen daily for 7 days.

If you resort back to old "diet thinking", if you perceive your weight loss sagging, you're creating a trap for yourself.

Enthusiasm, energy and determination are essential ingredients to progress. Set a realistic goal and give yourself something to aim for. Set your sights high, but be realistic.

READ-ALONG HYPNOSIS - STEP #3

The best way to benefit from the Slim for Life™ hypnosis experience is to upgrade to the full online program, which contains the audio tracks.

The following pages contain a version of the tracks converted into a "read-along" format, which will serve as a wonderful preview and jumpstart into what awaits you inside the full program.

~ ~ ~ ~ ~ ~ ~ ~

I recommend sitting comfortably and reading this hypnotic excerpt slowly, imagining that I'm speaking directly with you:

Take a moment to think again about how much weight you intend to release. Think about your target weight, your ideal size and perfect shape. Think about how good you will feel, how good you will look and how proud you can be achieving that slim, healthy body you deserve. Get that vision really clear in your mind.

Enjoy the feeling of allowing my words to register deep into the subconscious part of your mind as you become receptive to my suggestions which are entirely for your benefit and wellbeing.

Pay attention once again to your breathing. Allow yourself take a few deeper breaths and as you do so, imagine you're breathing in peace and tranquillity and releasing all tension. Breathing away all bad habits now as all unwanted thoughts, feelings and behaviours dissipate now.

As you relax, I'd like you to connect with that special part of you, the subconscious mind. This wonderful, beautiful, spiritual part of you has stored everything that has ever happened to you in this life experience and even before you were born. Your subconscious interacts with your conscious mind, higher consciousness (or spirit) and your physical body and has the great power to influence your conscious mind and your physical body and can today, focus on helping you to become completely free from the habits that in the past, have caused you to gain weight and prevented you from releasing excess weight quickly, easily and permanently.

You know, and I know that you know, you are now determined to release excess weight. You've decided to fix your problems, to get rid of certain habits, and I'd like your subconscious mind to know that I am quite impressed by your willingness to do so. After all, it isn't very easy to admit that you need help. It isn't easy to admit that you've dieted very many times and failed to correct these problems, yet. Though I'd like your subconscious mind to know that you certainly do have the ability to do so. I'm sure, because I've seen what people can achieve.

The people who cannot, do not go to the trouble, or expense, or invest their time and energy studying this Slim for Life philosophy. They just keep telling themselves that it is silly to seek help to do something they could do on their own anytime, anyplace, anywhere, just like that, overnight if they really put their mind to it, which of course they never seem to remember to do ... unlike you.

We both know you're here today because you really truly do want to get help. You really want to get rid of that habit and you've made your decision. Congratulations to you. You decided to do so, and it is none too soon, and it's definitely not too late; and I know you can change. I know you can stop. I know you can quit that behaviour because I have seen what people can do. Did you know too, there's even a program that helps schizophrenics, psychotics and people who are brain damaged too, to learn how to manage their behaviour which is very difficult for them?

It's a simple program, designed by a Dr. Abraham Zed. It consists of nothing more than writing down what they want to change. Then writing down each of the steps involved - the specific things they need to do to accomplish their goal. After that, they write down why. They write down why they should - the benefits of that change, as many advantages as they can think of.

They write them all down and then each and every day, they look at that thing they want to do and they look at the specific steps involved, and they look at why they want to do it, to remind themselves. All this writing everything down is quite necessary for them, absolutely necessary because they can't remember from one day to the next what it is they meant to do, or why they wanted to do it, or what they needed to do to accomplish that goal of being slim, healthy and happy for life through eating just the right amounts at just the right times. They can't remember it all at all, all because they are handicapped in some way.

Such a pleasure to be here with you, because I know that you will remember what you want to do, and why you want to do it, for you, and how to do it too. So I don't have to make you write it all down in detail or look at it each and every day, except in your mind, your unconscious mind perhaps. I can just ask you to think it all through, to define what you want to do exactly, to look at how to do it precisely, to do what you need to do each moment of each day. I know that you will remember it thoroughly later on, and I also know that I really don't need to tell you that you won't do that anymore, that you'll find it easier to not do it, all by yourself and you'll be reminding yourself.

Although, I could say to you in a way that will reach deep inside your mind and create an irresistible response, that no matter how hard you try, you'll never be able to over-eat again in exactly the same way, or at all without noticing exactly how ridiculous it seems to make you feel.

I could also say to you in a way that will reach deep into your mind and create an irresistible response that no matter how hard you try you'll never be able to over-drink again in exactly the same way, or at all without noticing exactly how unpleasant it seems to make you feel.

I could say to you in a way that will reach deep inside your mind and create an irresistible response that no matter how hard you try, you'll never be able to snack, or pick, or binge, or graze when you're not even hungry, again in exactly the same way, or at all without noticing how revolting it seems to make you feel. All of which you had probably overlooked before or forgot all about. However, not as much forgetting as the people I mentioned before who have a disability in that area, which is why they write it all down.

This all reminds me of a woman I saw on TV who forgot to live her life to the fullest. She went to work every day and stayed at home every night. She saved money for her and her husband's retirement when they would finally do what they wanted. However, when she retired she found out she had cancer and only a few months left to live. She cried as she talked and said she'd wasted her entire life putting off what she wanted to do. She'd ruined her life by forgetting to pay attention to what she did each day and each evening.

Thankfully, she created her own happy ending and decided to give herself strict orders to take good care of herself now; to be good to herself now, which is not the same as being forced to eat your greens, or told never to give yourself a treat but some people have to write it down before they get the point that now is the time to do what you can do, or cannot do that you have made the decision to do entirely for you.

So you can review your habits today with the full recognition that you can remember what to do and that not remembering is not something you'll find easy because now it belongs to you. Even after today it will be there with you, the memory of an ability to find a different way to do those things for you that it used to do but can't do now anymore, because now if you do it you'll be doing it on purpose and that's really not the same, is it?

You accept now, without the slightest reservation, the total responsibility for your body, your health, comfort, wellbeing, and happiness. You are now your own person - proud, confident and in control with that problem finally resolved.

And so before coming back from that place and returning to this place, I'd like you to take a moment to remember every positive thought you've ever had about yourself ... and smile ... How good does that feel?

Step #4: Boost Metabolism - Eat Less, Burn More

Increase your capacity to burn fat.

Improve the value of exercise - even walking.

Develop a sense of pride and accomplishment.

Crave moving your body more.

While listening to the hypnosis audio for Step #4 you'll experience another wonderful opportunity to enjoy the highly therapeutic process of going deep inside your mind, turning the world off to focus on your own wellbeing - a habit I really hope you're beginning to love!

Slim for Life Step #4: Boost Metabolism - Eat Less, Burn More will enable your subconscious mind to recognize how very easy it can be to eat smaller portions of healthy nutritious food while burning your calorific intake faster.

Perhaps you'll recognize "naughty" behaviour from the past - sneaking food while no-one's looking, being secretive or in denial about what you had, in the past been consuming. I recall the case of one client who admitted that while his wife was at home preparing a light evening dinner for them both, he'd stop on his way home from work to order a take-away, scoff quickly in the car and then go home and act as if he'd been starving himself since lunchtime!

Your subconscious mind can cause you to begin to feel an urge, a craving perhaps to move more, burning away the excess flab. Slim for Life really is a life-changing experience as you allow my suggestions to influence you.

You'll notice yourself genuinely feeling a lot calmer now with a sense of inner peace, security and clarity coming to the forefront, and noticing that somehow you're no longer stressing or obsessing about food. Food becomes quite an insignificant part of your daily routine.

The hypnotic suggestions will help to improve the value of exercise, even walking, as you find yourself craving getting out there, into the fresh air and embracing nature.

No more "I know I shouldn't ... but I'll eat it anyway." Increased energy levels perhaps seemingly coming from nowhere, but certainly due to you making better food choices and eating smaller portions of only healthy nutritious foods, that lead to improved health and wellbeing.

Gaining a real sense of having more confidence as you enjoy your journey to the body you desire, and no longer feeling trapped in a cage - a cage of your own making, which allows that feeling of freedom - lighter in all ways. How good does that feel?

Enjoy the hypnotic audio – and remember, for maximum effectiveness, listen daily for 7 days.

If you feel like giving up, think about why you started. You deserve to be slim, happy and healthy!

Your slim, healthy body is what makes you feel sexy. Your radiant smile shows your charisma. Your inner peace is what makes your true beauty shine.

Trust yourself to glow in harmony.

READ-ALONG HYPNOSIS – STEP #4

The best way to benefit from the Slim for Life™ hypnosis experience is to upgrade to the full online program, which contains the audio tracks.

The following pages contain a version of the tracks converted into a "read-along" format, which will serve as a wonderful preview and jumpstart into what awaits you inside the full program.

~ ~ ~ ~ ~ ~ ~ ~

I recommend sitting comfortably and reading this hypnotic excerpt slowly, imagining that I'm speaking directly with you:

Take a moment to think again about how much weight you intend to release. Think about your target weight, your ideal size and perfect shape. Think about how good you will feel, how good you will look and how proud you can be achieving that slim, healthy body you deserve. Get that vision really clear in your mind.

Enjoy the feeling of allowing my words to register deep into the subconscious part of your mind as you become receptive to my suggestions which are entirely for your benefit and wellbeing.

You are determined to achieve your goal of releasing that excess weight and allowing yourself to look and feel absolutely great. Taking a few deeper breaths now, and no matter what life's throwing at you at the moment, I'd love for you to allow yourself to enjoy some time focusing on wellbeing and simply imagining that you're breathing in peace and breathing away any cares and concerns.

You can notice that your body can relax and your mind can relax as I guide you to your goal. Allowing no tension at all to come into you focusing only on achieving the slim, healthy body that you desire, that you've set your heart on - Slim for Life.

Let's get started on your reason for reading today. For a while you have needed some help with your problems because, as you say, at times you just cannot help doing and thinking and eating and drinking the things that you do. I do know a bit about how it feels to be unable to stop. Every one of us knows a little bit about it because we've all tried to not cough, to not sneeze, to not yawn, to not scratch an itch. Though, I know that just scratches the very surface of what it is like for you to feel so, so ***v e r y*** uncomfortable that you have to do what you do to make it feel better. Or so it seems. However, you do know on the one hand and you have told yourself to stop, but none of that seems to have worked because what you are doing is not really you, even though it feels like it.

The more I think about this I have to wonder if you have ever seen a movie called "Aliens Snatch Bodies"? It's quite an odd story, where aliens invade human bodies. They somehow take them over, somehow get inside and take over their brains controlling them from the inside. In scene after scene people notice themselves doing some things that they would not do otherwise but they're unable to control themselves, because they are not themselves.

It seems they can still think clearly on the one hand, whereas on the other, their thoughts, their feelings, emotions and actions are controlled by the other. The aliens are in charge. It's like they're under some kind of spell that they do really well. They're still conscious and aware of everything going on but unable to control themselves. The challenge is in how to rebel and take charge again and when you go deep inside to really think about it you realize that there is always a way in all ways to find a happy outcome. It's one decision away, today to focus their energy, drive out that alien and take charge.

Then they decide to implement change, even if the force says "No." They decide to go, do whatever it is they are not supposed to do and refuse to do anything that alien is trying to do because they know, if they can just try, it just once will loosen its grip for a few moments and then do it again and again ... there's freedom on the other side.

With some determination to succeed it starts getting weaker - just a tiny bit at first and then eventually evaporates into nothing. It disappears into thin air and I always wonder just how it must feel to feel that happen, as that other source of thought, that other thing inside begins to let go and at last you feel that feeling of the freedom, to think for yourself and let wellbeing take over once and for all.

I know you've been wishing, hoping, wanting, praying even, for many years to say the last word on this weight loss subject. You've maybe spent a lifetime arming yourself with final words and you can drift away on my words, recalling that last word you really want to say now that you have the chance. Chances are, as you take this valuable time to focus on your wellbeing that you'll recognize some part of you that's only just begun to find its voice. Can you hear it? What's it saying to you now? I believe it's a voice of self-confidence, self-belief, yes belief in yourself at last, and belief in your ability to achieve your weight goal. I believe you can hear belief in your ability to solve this problem once and for all, to exercise your privilege and your right to have the body you desire, the body you deserve, the body you've dreamed all about - slim, healthy and happy ... Slim for Life.

I'd love for you to offer yourself large portions of self-confidence, huge portions of self-absorption, enormous helpings of self-esteem, and gigantic portions of self-love as your subconscious mind takes some time to understand, acknowledge and express the words and the melody of your personal body song.

Carefully listen to and monitor yourself, nurture yourself, take really good care of yourself in every way. You are gaining each day in self-confidence, improving body-confidence, learning the skill of self-knowledge and recognizing feelings of self-worth as you enjoy shaping your body into its richest, sweetest tones while, all the while toning it down.

From this day forward, eating is purely for pleasure. Perhaps you'd forgotten how to experience the pleasure of feeling hungry, the contentment of feeling full, the satisfaction in feeling satisfied and the sheer pleasure of taking control of yourself and your life.

Connect with the fun of saying "No… thank you." Maybe you eat a lot, maybe you don't eat a lot of the right foods, maybe you simply don't eat much at all, but I'm sure you're not getting much pleasure. You can eat less and get more pleasure. You can want less and have more pleasure. You can heighten your metabolism to enjoy feeling a sense of warmth caressing your skin, spreading through your entire body through your arms, legs and flowing from the top of your head down through to the tips of your fingers and the tips of your toes as you enjoy the glorious pleasure of 'less is more'.

Experiencing that increased energy warming and enthusing you all over as you embrace the feeling, the pleasure of achieving the slim, happy, healthy body you desire. Recalling that time in your life when you know how beautiful you are, recognizing that fountain of knowledge you have and expressing your mind once and for all as your reserve of last words, your melody and your body song is finally voiced, as you become even more determined than ever before to hear your inner voice.

Aah ... how good does that feel? Take a moment to really notice just how good that feels!

This new vision of yourself can replace the earlier one because it is a new representation of you, a new version of you that is so confident and relaxed that success comes quite naturally. Feel that now and let it bring about a state of mind of being able to achieve everything you want in life. You are Slim for Life.

You accept now, without the slightest reservation, the total responsibility for your body, your health, comfort, wellbeing, and happiness. You are now your own person - proud, confident and in control with that problem finally resolved.

And so before coming back from that place and returning to this place, I'd like you to take a moment to remember every positive thought you've ever had about yourself ... and smile ... How good does that feel?

Step #5: A Slimmer You

Visualization technique.

See yourself slim. Feel thinner.

Develop the thought processes and habits of a naturally slender, healthy person.

While listening to the hypnosis audio for Step #5 the meditative process will promote a feeling of whole mind and body balance and freedom to believe and achieve your weight release goal.

Slim for Life Step #5: A Slimmer You is a visualisation technique that facilitates your subconscious mind in actually seeing you thinner, feeling slender and really getting into that zone. It will cause your mind to "believe" that you've already achieved your target size and weight - a true recognition of precisely how good you'll look and feel, and of what others will think and say about the new you. As you follow this part of the process, your subconscious, believing you're already there, will exaggerate those of my suggestions which benefit you the most and adjust your intake, thoughts, feelings and emotions to the person you're visualising - the new you.

Tasting food in your mind, tuning into your senses and noticing that somewhat strangely perhaps, you dislike the taste of some things you used to think you enjoyed. Allowing the power of your subconscious mind to do its best work for you and supporting this life-changing experience as you now step into your new slim, healthy body. It's ALL about you.

As Thomas Troward put it in his wonderful essay, *Entering Into the Spirit of It:*

"That point where struggles and anxieties are released, as perfect rest becomes one with ceaseless activity."

You don't need to try hard, simply allow the changes to take place, as calm and inner peace becomes mixed with even greater feelings of determination to succeed.

Less mind chatter and more clarity as you take control of your life, your feelings, your emotions as well as your food, and recognizing that it's not so much about what you eat that's important, but more about what you think about what you eat, and you are no longer willing to allow others prevent your progress.

Taking even greater control as you adjust to petite-sized portions whether you're eating at home or out. Eating, drinking and exercising for that slimmer body, even before it manifests physically. Increased energy levels, boosted metabolism, improved health, sleeping well and enjoying, observing, embracing and developing the habits of a naturally slim person as a newfound courage, confidence and deep sense of pride you become the new you!

Enjoy the hypnotic audio - and remember, for maximum effectiveness, listen daily for 7 days.

Discipline: The art of giving yourself a command and following it through. Hold the image in your mind of you having achieved your goal.

Remember your Goal Card!

Continue your journey. Stick to your goal. Learn from your mistakes.

You can do it - I know you can - because I've seen what people just like you have achieved!

READ-ALONG HYPNOSIS – STEP #5

The best way to benefit from the Slim for Life™ hypnosis experience is to upgrade to the full online program, which contains the audio tracks.

The following pages contain a version of the tracks converted into a "read-along" format, which will serve as a wonderful preview and jumpstart into what awaits you inside the full program.

~ ~ ~ ~ ~ ~ ~ ~

I recommend sitting comfortably and reading this hypnotic excerpt slowly, imagining that I'm speaking directly with you:

Take a moment to think again about how much weight you intend to release. Think about your target weight, your ideal size and perfect shape. Think about how good you will feel, how good you will look and how proud you can be achieving that slim, healthy body you deserve. Get that vision really clear in your mind.

Enjoy the feeling of allowing my words to register deep into the subconscious part of your mind as you become receptive to my suggestions which are entirely for your benefit and wellbeing.

Make yourself comfortable and again notice your breathing. Imagine that you're breathing in peace and harmony and with each easy outward breath, releasing unwanted thoughts, feelings and behaviours as you allow yourself to relax while you focus on your goal ... being Slim for Life.

As an exercise for the imagination, take a moment to imagine that you are in a restaurant. You're sitting in a restaurant observing some slim people looking through the menu. What are they doing? In their minds they are actually tasting the food, taking their time and visualizing how it will look served on the plate. They're thinking about the flavours, colours and the nutritional value. They're tasting the combinations in their minds. What they are not thinking about is how comfortable they will feel. Now, what I'd like you to be thinking about is yourself at your desired size and weight. Think about how good you will feel about yourself, how good you will look and what you are wearing. Take a moment to imagine what your friends and family will think about how good you look.

During this Slim for Life program it's important to recognize that you are developing the habits of naturally slim people - those seemingly lucky people who seem to eat what they want, yet maintain a slim, healthy body.

I'm going to suggest that there is absolutely no reason whatsoever for you to be surprised at how quickly and easily you can release all excess weight. Just visualize now your goal. Think about how proud you will feel lighter, slimmer, fitter, healthier, more energetic and filled with the vitality of life ... lighter in all ways. How good does that feel?

Great; and continuing to exercise your imagination, I want you to recall a special and very pleasant memory of yours from the past. There may be a few, but your subconscious mind will understand and select one that's of significance to you now. Unconsciously you know it is of value to you now, as you experience those successful feelings now. For you know that the answers come from that memory held way back then.

That's good… now, in your mind, in your imagination I want you to go to a special room; a room of resourcefulness, of belief and of capability. In this room you notice there's only one item and that is a television. Good, because as you look at that television, what I would like you to do is to put onto the blank screen of that television all of that excess weight that you have, that you want to release permanently. Put it all up there on that screen, all of those extra fat cells. Perhaps you can see them as pinkish in colour, perhaps orange, or maybe they're grey, all piled up on that screen as an ugly fatty mass.

Now add to the screen just how uncomfortable you feel when you over-eat and over-drink especially fizzy drinks, sodas, alcohol and eat junk foods, take-aways and pick and snack and graze when you're not even hungry and all that extra... indulgence... well you know what belongs here. Now put into the picture what your family and friends think about you being overweight. Add into the picture all of the reasons that you have for your need to over-eat … be it lack of love, unhappiness, stress, problems from childhood and all of that emotional stuff that in the past has taken you off track. Whatever those reasons, your subconscious mind knows exactly what is meant here so add it all there to that screen. Now put onto that screen all of the damage that over-eating, or not eating or drinking enough of the right things, consuming all that unhealthy fattening produce does to your body.

Maybe you'll include high cholesterol, high blood pressure, breathlessness, the danger of heart attack and stroke, the risk of diabetes, depressive thought patterns that come to the forefront of your mind when you know you've gorged … that uncomfortable feeling when you over-eat … and any other health concerns you may be experiencing. Add any feelings of guilt and disgust, feelings of shame that you are not taking on the responsibility for your own health and wellbeing carrying all that excess weight. This is very powerful so get that picture really clearly in your mind now.

Well done; now please store this picture somewhere convenient in your mind because we will need it later.

Okay, that's good. I want you now to see another picture there on that television screen. It's a smaller inset picture in the top right of the screen. Make this picture one of you now having released all of that excess weight so you're looking and feeling noticeably lighter, wearing the new clothes you'd like to wear with the slim, healthy, happy body you know is within your grasp. In this picture, notice how good you feel. Notice how good you look and feel, that growing feeling of self-confidence, increased self-esteem… you are happier, healthier, more alive and lighter in all ways. This is you taking great care of you and with that feeling of huge optimism and determination to succeed at becoming Slim for Life.

Assess yourself in this picture on a scale of one to ten, for self-confidence a ten, for self-esteem a ten, ten for self-respect, self-love: ten. This is the version of you who eats only when your appetite tells you that you are hungry, stops eating when your appetite tells you that it is full, a friend of your appetite, fully aware that on your tongue are thousands of taste buds and when you put food into your mouth they will very quickly become satisfied. This is the version of you who chews food slowly and thoroughly and carefully until your appetite is satisfied, accepting that any more food than is enough to satisfy your appetite is waste. That waste can either be wasted in the garbage or wasted on your waist - waste or waist. Which will you choose?

In a moment as you watch that television screen you will imagine hearing me say the word WHOOSH and you can make that small picture grow, spread across the screen - that picture of the new you. You will do this very fast and you will do it multiple times as this is how the subconscious mind learns. WHOOSH ... erasing all of those old eating and drinking habits ... WHOOSHING, releasing, erasing all of that excess weight, all of that discomfort, that feeling of disgust, guilt, shame ... until that picture fills the screen eliminating completely that old picture and filling the screen with the new you.

Now make the screen go blank and put back the old picture. Notice what is different about it and put back the inset picture in the top right corner of the screen and now WHOOSH again ... WHOOSHING ... erasing that old you, releasing, eliminating that excess weight ... WHOOSHING ... erasing all of those feelings of discomfort, of lack of confidence; eliminating feelings of guilt and all of those unhelpful eating and drinking habits, all of those negative thoughts and feelings erased and eliminated as the new you fills the screen completely now.

Now make the screen go blank and put back the old picture onto the screen. Notice what's different and really take your time as this is important. Look at the colour now and notice all of the changes. Now ... WHOOSH again, WHOOSHING, releasing, erasing that old you ... eliminating that excess weight and WHOOSHING ...

erasing all those feelings of discomfort, of lack of self-confidence, lack of body confidence, eliminating those feelings of self-disgust, guilt and all of those bad eating and drinking habits; all of those negative thoughts, feelings and emotions erased and eliminated as the new you fills the screen completely now.

Now walk over to that television and turn up the brightness, turn it up as high as it will go and WHOOSH again, WHOOSHING … erasing all of those feelings of discomfort, lack of confidence … WHOOSHING … erasing that old you, releasing all excess weight, eliminating those feelings of self-hatred and guilt; all those sad, bad, over-eating unhealthy fattening food habits, all of those bad over-drinking, fattening and unhealthy drink habits, all of those negative feelings erased and eliminated as the new you fills the screen completely now.

Now make the screen go blank and put on it all that remains of that old picture - the small remains; the crumbs; the dregs of that old picture; the smallest traces and WHOOSH again … erasing all that remains of that old picture, all that remains of those old overeating habits, those sad, bad feelings, releasing completely all of that excess weight, those feelings of discomfort, as the new and exciting, slimmer, healthier, happier you fills the screen completely. See the new and so confident you, the considerably lighter, healthier, happier and more energetic you filling that screen completely now in full and glorious colour. How good do you look? How incredible do you feel? Let those wonderful feelings expand and grow! Yes , I know!

Now step into that picture ... into that television ... and try out that new body. Step into the new you - Slim for Life, smiling, self-confident you. Having released that excess weight now and striding out - happy, smiling, looking and feeling SO good. Are you oozing with pride, confidence, charisma? Wearing gorgeous new clothes? Yes! Walk around now and experience fully that new slender body and become familiar with the new you.

Ah ... I love it! And so, I'd like to ask your subconscious mind to re-enforce every single positive thought you've ever had about yourself and re-enforce every suggestion you have heard me utter.

You accept now, without the slightest reservation, the total responsibility for your body, your health, comfort, wellbeing, and happiness. You are now your own person - proud, confident and in control with that problem finally resolved.

And so before coming back from that place and returning to this place, I'd like you to take a moment to remember every positive thought you've ever had about yourself ... and smile ... How good does that feel?

Step #6: Hypno-Gastric Band

Virtual surgery – Gastric Band surgery without actually going under the knife!

While listening to the hypnosis audio for Step #6 you'll experience again a deeply therapeutic hypnotic process that enhances feelings of inner peace, almost perhaps, a feeling of letting someone else take the driving seat for a moment.

Slim for Life Step #6: Hypno-Gastric Band - virtual surgery without actually going under the knife, takes your mind through a virtual operation. As part of the Slim for Life course this is considered to be even more effective than physical surgery. That's a bold statement but I've worked with many clients who've been through physical surgery and not only did it not work, but in some cases it caused illness. Mindset is everything!

I recall some clients who came to my clinic for help. Prior to her physical surgery, Marie regularly ate a whole pack of currant buns with butter and jam for breakfast. That's 6 buns laden with sugar, every morning for breakfast. Christine and Joe, husband and wife - one would eat 4 slices of toasted bread and the other a pot of raw cake mix while preparing their dinner each evening. Terry, while his wife was at home preparing him a deliciously healthy salad for dinner would stop every evening on his way home from work to first eat a take-out pizza with fries. Following physical gastric band surgery each of these clients followed those same bad habits, filling their stomachs with unhealthy produce, leaving no room for anything nutritious and ultimately leading to a variety of illnesses.

A complete mind and body makeover is the only way so prepare yourself for using your mind for change.

In Step #6 once again you'll go deep inside your mind, turn the world off and enjoy this life-changing surgical experience. Another extremely important aspect in this Slim for Life program as the feeling of whole mind and body relaxation continues to promote healing, feelings of calm and a greater sense of security.

Some clients report that while listening they can feel a slight tension in their abdomen while the surgeon performs his art, and afterwards, a physical feeling that the 'surgery' has actually taken place in the physical world.

Afterwards you'll find yourself craving only very tiny portions of healthy nutritious food and tuning into the ways that the nutrition, vitamins and minerals are influencing your mind and your body.

Amazingly you'll begin noticing that you really are full after just a few mouthfuls and the increased energy levels cause you to crave moving your body more. You are recognizing that the more you use it, the more easily you lose it - In other words, the more quickly you'll release ALL of that excess weight!

The result is improved health and wellbeing, improved longevity and through taking control, increased feelings of self-confidence and self-worth.

Enjoy the hypnotic audio - and remember, for maximum effectiveness, listen daily for 7 days.

How people treat others is a direct reflection of how they feel about themselves. Stop listening to anyone and anything that gets you off track.

Act like you have complete faith in yourself - Your subconscious mind will soon start to believe it!

READ-ALONG HYPNOSIS – STEP #6

The best way to benefit from the Slim for Life™ hypnosis experience is to upgrade to the full online program, which contains the audio tracks.

The following pages contain a version of the tracks converted into a "read-along" format, which will serve as a wonderful preview and jumpstart into what awaits you inside the full program.

~ ~ ~ ~ ~ ~ ~ ~

I recommend sitting comfortably and reading this hypnotic excerpt slowly, imagining that I'm speaking directly with you:

Take a moment to think again about how much weight you intend to release. Think about your target weight, your ideal size and perfect shape. Think about how good you will feel, how good you will look and how proud you can be achieving that slim, healthy body you deserve. Get that vision really clear in your mind.

Enjoy the feeling of allowing my words to register deep into the subconscious part of your mind as you become receptive to my suggestions which are entirely for your benefit and wellbeing.

I really hope you're beginning to enjoy the powerful hypnotic content, as once again you go deep inside your mind to turn the world off and focus on personal wellbeing. Allowing all tension to leave your body now as you relax deeply and begin to feel more in control of your life, in control of your mind and your body and connected with your own sense of inner wisdom.

Take a few deeper breaths now and as you do so, I would like you to imagine you're breathing in peace ... and as you breathe out, breathe away all cares and concerns. As each word you read and each easy gentle breath moves you closer and closer to your weight release goal.

Notice that your body can relax, and your mind can relax, and your mind has become very sensitive to my suggestions that will help you the most and you allow no tension at all to come into you.

Today we're going on an imaginative journey whereby you can use the power of your wise subconscious mind to assist in releasing all that excess weight that you've been carrying around for so long. You are becoming more and more determined to improve your life, to be Slim for Life and for this reason you have decided to use gastric band hypnosis to help you. You have seen, heard, and read the success stories of others who have lost weight through this method and you are absolutely determined to join them and become your own success story. You feel sure this is the best route for you to release excess weight permanently. Hypno-Gastric Band is even safer and more effective than physical surgery because you can undergo this operation without having to go 'under the knife'.

Using the power of your imagination, I'd like you to visualize the things I suggest to the very best of your ability. Make the images real and notice any sensory information that accompanies your impressions. Imagine that you have chosen the clinic or hospital where this procedure is to take place and you are seated now in the doctor's office undergoing your first consultation. The doctor is very kind and friendly and immediately puts you at ease. He understands and supports your decision. You discuss exactly how much weight you want to release. Tell the doctor now your target weight and your target size. Explain your personal reasons for your decision to become Slim for Life. What does this mean for you, in the future? He listens attentively and tells you that obesity isn't something to be ashamed of as it is an illness, a disease which can be treated very successfully by using this method.

You listen carefully as the doctor provides you with all the facts. You will have the operation by keyhole surgery and will probably be able to go home the same day. There will be a couple of follow-up appointments in the weeks ahead where you will be X-rayed to see if the band needs to be adjusted slightly.

The doctor tells you that when you've had the operation it is important to eat slowly and chew your food thoroughly, allowing the enzymes in your mouth to break down the food. This aids the digestive process and you'll find yourself becoming full very quickly. Interestingly, you'll begin to notice that you enjoy your food more than ever before. He explains that there are thousands of taste buds in your mouth, and you'll notice that certain foods that you used to eat won't appeal to you anymore - especially dairy products, sugar, cakes, buns and cookies; snacks like crisps, potato chips, and also bread and potatoes. Instead, you'll notice you crave fresh food, especially fruits and vegetables.

You really want to go through with this surgery. It's a life-changing process and you can't wait to release all that excess weight. You've waited long enough. You leave the clinic feeling happy and optimistic.

Now, project your mind into the future. Imagine now that it's time for you to go for your surgery. You've been on a liquid-only diet for two weeks in preparation for your operation. Since last night you've been fasting, so you've not eaten or drunk anything since before bed last night. You arrive at the clinic and check in at the reception desk and are warmly welcomed into your room. There's a gown for you to change into and as you browse a magazine you notice how relaxed you feel.

After a short time, a man in a green gown enters your room introducing himself to you as your anaesthetist. He asks you a few questions and explains the procedure. His visit is followed by the surgeon who gives you a few tips about what to expect after your operation. He explains that they will provide you with healthy eating guides and information on different activities which will be beneficial for you, recommending walking for at least half an hour every day, even twice per day and perhaps swimming or cycling.

The healthy eating guides won't be an issue for you because you won't want to eat junk foods and you won't be able to overeat - the gastric band will make sure of that. He tells you to make friends with your band and help it to do its job for you in supporting you in releasing excess weight to achieve a slim, healthy body. How good will that feel? You are reminded to aid the digestive process by eating slowly to enable your saliva to break down the food quickly and easily.

Despite what lies ahead, you don't feel the least bit nervous ... on the contrary, you're excited for your new, healthy, happy body. The anaesthetist greets you again and before you know it, you're closing your eyes and counting, drifting down from ten, nine, eight... feeling totally relaxed; even with the bright lights overhead, you are beginning to feel quite sleepy ...

... your eyes are tightly closed and you feel at ease.

The surgeon is very skilled, having performed this keyhole surgery many times before. He makes a few small incisions in the abdomen and gently inserts his laparoscope. It's a thin, rigid tube which contains a light and a tiny camera that relays images of the inside of your abdomen to a television screen to ensure absolute accuracy for the job at hand. Your subconscious mind is fully aware of exactly what is happening, but you don't feel any discomfort at all. From now on, after just a few small mouthfuls you'll begin to feel full.

The surgeon carefully manoeuvres the band into position and now your stomach is the size of a small tennis ball. As you adjust your eating habits, you will find that you are only able to enjoy small portions of healthy, nutritious food.

The procedure is almost over and while the surgeon stitches the wound you feel so comfortably relaxed - and you begin to drift off into a deep hypnotic, restful sleep. After a while you open your eyes and look around, wondering at first where you are; and then you remember your gastric band surgery. The anaesthetic has started to wear off a little and while there's a slight discomfort, but it's easily bearable.

The operation went perfectly, just as you knew it would and after a few checks, you leave the hospital feeling happy. Time to eat something now, but amazingly, after just a few nibbles you find that you are already full. From now on it's the same with every meal. You eat smaller and smaller portions, finding that you are so easily satisfied that you just don't want any more food. You are eating slowly and really chewing your food thoroughly before swallowing and noticing you find that you can't eat anywhere near as much as you used to. In a strange way, you no longer crave chocolate, biscuits, buns, cakes, bread and snacks. You just don't enjoy eating junk food anymore – it seems tasteless.

Over the next few days and weeks you find yourself feeling hungry much less often and eating very small portions of only clean, healthy, nutritious food. You're eating slowly, chewing thoroughly and reaching that feeling of being full very quickly.

The excess weight is dropping off you. Before long, you feel lighter in all ways as you're releasing weight - feeling slimmer, healthier and happier, and noticing a real sense of pride as you grow each day in self-confidence, body-confidence and self-respect. Realizing it's all due to your gastric band operation, you feel more motivated, craving getting out into the fresh air and craving walking, swimming, moving your new body and becoming more and more aware that the more you use it the more quickly you lose it … you're heading with ease towards that slim, healthy, happy body you deserve ... Slim for Life.

From this day forward, the memory of this gastric band surgery can remain vivid and clear as though it has occurred in your physical life so that whenever you see those products which are unhealthy and you know will pile on the pounds, your subconscious mind can remind you, in a manner that is instant and powerful, of your commitment to yourself and to your decision to be Slim for Life.

You accept now, without the slightest reservation, the total responsibility for your body, your health, comfort, wellbeing, and happiness. You are now your own person - proud, confident and in control with that problem finally resolved.

And so before coming back from that place and returning to this place, I'd like you to take a moment to remember every positive thought you've ever had about yourself ... and smile ... How good does that feel?

Step #7: Release Negative Emotions and Build Self-Esteem

Stop emotional and comfort eating.

Let go of the past. Forgive yourself and others.

Improve feelings of self-worth.

Recognize that you do deserve to be slim.

While listening to the hypnosis audio for Step #7 you'll experience a deeply therapeutic hypnotic process that encourages whole mind and body relaxation and recognition that you have the ability to go deep inside your mind and find inner peace anytime you want to and choose those thoughts you accept and/or reject.

Slim for Life Step #7: Release Negative Emotions and Build Self-Esteem supports your weight release goal by working directly with, and easing any of, your emotions that may be counter-productive to releasing excess weight. For example: frustration, anger, anxiety, guilt, revenge, and any other of the lower emotions.

You'll experience a greater perspective and rationalization of difficult situations and a process of letting go as you fully release all unwanted, unhelpful thought patterns to allow forgiveness of yourself and others.

Recognizing that you deserve to be Slim for Life and are worthy of this life-changing experience. Feelings of calm, security and perfect inner peace become your reality as you sense a release from the past and taking control of the "now." Dealing more easily with everyday problems large or small without feeling overwhelmed.

No longer letting things get to you enables improved feelings of self-worth as you experience an end to emotional or comfort eating and drinking. Increasing energy levels become feelings of empowerment. Taking ownership of your improved health and sleeping soundly, waking up refreshed, noticing a powerful connection between your mind and your body that promotes self-confidence, higher self-esteem and sense of pride in simply being the best version of you!

Enjoy the hypnotic audio – and remember, for maximum effectiveness, listen daily for 7 days.

*"Never give up on a dream
just because of the time
it will take to accomplish it.
The time will pass anyway."*
~ Earl Nightingale

READ-ALONG HYPNOSIS – STEP #7

The best way to benefit from the Slim for Life™ hypnosis experience is to upgrade to the full online program, which contains the audio tracks.

The following pages contain a version of the tracks converted into a "read-along" format, which will serve as a wonderful preview and jumpstart into what awaits you inside the full program.

~ ~ ~ ~ ~ ~ ~ ~

I recommend sitting comfortably and reading this hypnotic excerpt slowly, imagining that I'm speaking directly with you:

Take a moment to think again about how much weight you intend to release. Think about your target weight, your ideal size and perfect shape. Think about how good you will feel, how good you will look and how proud you can be achieving that slim, healthy body you deserve. Get that vision really clear in your mind.

Enjoy the feeling of allowing my words to register deep into the subconscious part of your mind as you become receptive to my suggestions which are entirely for your benefit and wellbeing.

Once again, I'd like to imagine that you're breathing in peace and tranquillity, and with each easy outward breath release feelings of stress, worry and self-doubt. This is your time now with nobody wanting anything, expecting or needing anything. It's a time to relax and become completely focused on your own personal wellbeing.

Today is an opportunity to release all kinds of negative thoughts, feelings, behaviours and emotions - an experience of letting go of any thought patterns that may have, in the past, held you back from achieving the slim, happy, healthy body that you desire ... Slim for Life.

I'd like you to become aware that negative thoughts, negative feelings and negative emotions never change anything. They are simply a waste of energy and a lost opportunity to generate beneficial emotions and positive thoughts and feelings that will help you, serve you and support you in achieving your goal. Negative emotions are hurtful; they hurt you, they harm you, they cause you upset and pain. They actually do damage you and injure you because they are then expressed through the body, causing a variety of physical issues including excess weight.

When you experience any of the lower emotions such as fear or anxiety, hatred, anger, frustration, guilt, regret, jealousy, revenge or anything else you can add to this subject, this is because you are not getting something that you desire. Agree with yourself right now to stop wanting things that you know you cannot have. As you do this for yourself immediately you will become happier, more thankful and more contented with what you do have.

Agree now to change the way that you think about things. Longing for things that you do not have or cannot have, is ignoring and wasting the benefits, perfect health and wellbeing, happiness, and the slim, healthy body you desire, that are to be enjoyed with what you do have.

Begin now to practice feeling and expressing a sense of gratitude for what you do have. I completely understand that there are probably many things in your life that you would like to change or improve upon, but if you can take on board my suggestions here, you will reach your Slim for Life goal more quickly and easily. Express your gratitude for you and for your beautiful life. Be thankful for your friends and family, Mother Nature, neighbours, colleagues and strangers. Acknowledge and appreciate your health, your job, people, situations good and bad, and the amazing opportunities that are all around you if you're willing to notice them.

Appreciate the Slim for Life philosophy that's leading you to the slim, healthy body you're aiming for. Be thankful for clear blue skies and white fluffy clouds. Practice finding the beauty in a raindrop and the breeze through the trees. Make a decision to enjoy and be happy and thankful with what you do have.

If you are harbouring now any negative thoughts and feelings towards others, these only do you harm; they actually do cause you harm and pain. They only damage you. Negative thoughts and negative feelings hold you back in the past, keeping you precisely where you are now. Negative thoughts, feelings and emotions prevent you from moving forward, making progress, achieving your dreams, and making the most of your life. They prevent you from achieving your worthwhile goal of releasing all excess weight to allow yourself to feel absolutely great and achieve that slim, healthy, happy body that you dream of.

If you are harbouring any negative emotions, maybe all, or any of the lower emotions such as fear, anxiety, anger, frustration or jealousy, release these feelings, release these negative harmful emotions now. Let them all go and forever free yourself from what has been and is now no more. If you have sadness perhaps for something or someone that you have lost, grieve now for what you have lost, or for what you never had, and release that longing; release that craving ... just let go.

If you hold any feelings of guilt for something that you did, or perhaps for something that you omitted to do, forgive yourself; do it now and just let it all go. You have always done your best in any situation. You did what was right for you at the time, or you did what you did because it was all that you could do, with the skills and resources you had at the time. That's the past now, so allow yourself to release all feelings of guilt right now, release them whole-heartedly ... let them all go.

You have done your best, no matter what the situation. If you are holding feelings of fear, feelings of betrayal, jealousy or revenge, you can recognize now with clarity and understanding that those feelings really do not benefit you in any way. They hurt you and prevent you from concentrating your best efforts on enjoying and being thankful for what you do have - love, kindness, warmth, friendship and so much more, and you release those negative harmful emotions ... just let them go now ... they have no place in your life.

Your subconscious mind will help you with enjoying new positive thoughts and emotions. It will remind you in a very powerful manner whenever you experience any of the lower emotions that you have a choice and you can control your thoughts and feelings.

Decide to have only good thoughts and positive feelings and emotions. In the future, you will be aware when you experience a negative thought or emotion and you will immediately turn it into a positive thought or emotion that helps you to move forward and enjoy your life and be thankful for who you are and what you have.

You can become more and more aware of your own assets, the fine qualities and beauty within you ... taking control of your life and your health and making decisions that are in alignment with your Slim for Life goal. You are strong, self-confident, self-assured and worthy. Decisions that you have been putting off are easier now because you trust your own judgement and your ability to take control of your health, making decisions which are the right ones for you and those whom you love. You acknowledge your inner strength, wisdom, capabilities and capacities to put your health and wellbeing at the top of your agenda. You're beginning to recognize that the better you feel, the more resourceful you become. You admire yourself and love yourself so much more - and this is not in an egotistical way, but in a way that is positive, nurturing, natural and constructive.

Changes for the better are happening within you. Some you will be aware of now, while others may not become noticeable until sometime in the future.

Know and believe that whatever the mind can conceive and believe, can be achieved. Whatever you believe you can achieve, you will achieve. If you're struggling with self-belief, borrow my belief in you ... I believe you will achieve that slim, healthy body as from this day forward you enjoy the feeling of liking yourself and acknowledging all those fine aspects of you ... Mmmm ... how good do you feel?

You accept now, without the slightest reservation the total responsibility for your body, your health, comfort, wellbeing, and happiness. You are now your own person - proud, confident and in control with that problem finally resolved.

And so before coming back from that place and returning to this place, I'd like you to take a moment to remember every positive thought you've ever had about yourself ... and smile ... How good does that feel?

Step #8: Increase Motivation – Keep Going

Encouragement and motivation to move these ideas forward.

Eliminate fear of failure.

Recognize that all your worthwhile goals are achievable.

While listening to the hypnosis audio for Step #8 again you'll experience a deeply therapeutic, hypnotic process that promotes a feeling of whole mind and body relaxation to move you closer to your goal.

Slim for Life Step #8: Increase Motivation really helps to keep the momentum going. It supports, nurtures and encourages you in moving your new habits around food forward while eliminating that sometimes challenging, nagging, menacing voice that perhaps is saying "well ... you're not there yet" or "mmm ... well you've done all that effort, and it's not showing yet." It helps in releasing negative thought patterns around self-criticism.

You'll experience once again a thoroughly enjoyable, deeply therapeutic meditative process and while you go inside your mind and turn the world off at will, you'll begin to notice feelings of encouragement that come from within - from within your own subconscious mind.

This kind support is empowering, motivating and strengthens the ideas in this Slim for Life course to take you forward into achieving the body you desire - slim and healthy for life. It reinforces this life-changing process causing an even greater sense of being on track.

Elimination of the fears of failure, hopelessness, helplessness, as you find clarity and take control of your thoughts, recognizing that you own this very important goal - it belongs to you and nothing is going to stand in your way.

You are releasing excess weight. You are allowing yourself to feel absolutely great and a deep, powerful connection with your higher self, with who you really are as a result of your being in this life experience. Enjoying feelings of pride and accomplishment, assertion and dogged determination to succeed, while balancing energy levels, improving health, sleeping in a truly relaxed frame of mind and feeling more nourished from sleep, as while you slumber that gentle connection between your mind and your body promotes deep, deep inner healing. How good does that feel?

Enjoy the hypnotic audio - and remember, for maximum effectiveness, listen daily for 7 days.

> “*Whatever the mind of man can conceive and believe, it can achieve.*”
> *~ Napoleon Hill*

Start really believing in yourself right away!

READ-ALONG HYPNOSIS – STEP #8

The best way to benefit from the Slim for Life™ hypnosis experience is to upgrade to the full online program, which contains the audio tracks.

The following pages contain a version of the tracks converted into a "read-along" format, which will serve as a wonderful preview and jumpstart into what awaits you inside the full program.

~ ~ ~ ~ ~ ~ ~ ~

I recommend sitting comfortably and reading this hypnotic excerpt slowly, imagining that I'm speaking directly with you:

Take a moment to think again about how much weight you intend to release. Think about your target weight, your ideal size and perfect shape. Think about how good you will feel, how good you will look and how proud you can be achieving that slim, healthy body you deserve. Get that vision really clear in your mind.

Enjoy the feeling of allowing my words to register deep into the subconscious part of your mind as you become receptive to my suggestions which are entirely for your benefit and wellbeing.

I'd like you to allow yourself to take a few deep breaths while you imagine that you're breathing in peace and harmony, and with each outward breath release all unwanted, unhelpful thoughts, feelings and behaviours.

Let us contemplate the idea that a belief … is simply a thought … that we keep thinking.

While you relax here today, your mind automatically moves toward all those thoughts, beliefs, ideas, images, feelings and emotions that can clarify very clearly for you, the very things that you know that you know and you know that you do, that seem to get in the way. Your awareness can contemplate those things that need attention in precisely the same way that animals migrate. They act instinctively, automatically, intuitively, without thinking or trying. They somehow seem to know where to go and when, and what to do to take the utmost care of themselves. It's like a sort of inner voice, an inner awareness that moves the birds, the butterflies, the whales and whole herds of animals from one place to another. It only takes a change in temperature, a scent in the air, some sort of feeling that makes them restless as if something's not right that draws their attention toward that uncomfortable feeling. It sets them in motion, moving toward a new place, perhaps the ocean, like an expansive inner space of quiet comfort and effortless relaxation.

They'll move hundreds of miles, even thousands of miles, taking care of their young, taking care of themselves and each other. It's interesting, because everyone thinks that no one really knows exactly how it feels to be a butterfly that suddenly knows the time is right to exit that cocoon. It's time for a change, freedom for a change, and it certainly knows the exact change needed. Nobody knows, but they do know and so do you, just like you know when you are uncomfortable, or hungry or full.

We can relax and allow the imagination to know how it might feel to gradually or suddenly sense or feel that feeling, that inner awareness, maybe a restless recognition, that something needs to change now. We can follow through and allow actions to flow from those feelings as we respond effortlessly, easily to that inner knowing, that somehow tells us what to do and when and how to do it.

We, likewise, have an inner intuition, a subtle inner voice that we too often ignore. It knows what is good for us and what is a mistake, and everything becomes easier and effortless when we allow ourselves to listen attentively and trust our own judgement. When we do this we're guided, directed to our path of least resistance, and you can listen now as your path to your slim, healthy, happy body is revealed to you.

While you contemplate my words you may sense a kind of irresistible urge, a driving desire to do many of those things you complain you keep putting off. Remaining in this beautiful state of inner peace you may find great satisfaction in doing those things you haven't, and that nothing else is more fun. You could try to fight that impulse, reject my suggestions, all of which are for your benefit and wellbeing; and to not do anything for a while, if you can … or to not do them very well, if you must. So I am going to suggest that you go ahead and do some things, but just those things you really have to do. Only do what you need to do and try to force yourself to put off everything else so that my hypnotic suggestions have plenty of time to build up in force. Resist them as much as possible and just do some things, whatever things you feel you have to do but keep on fighting that hypnotic urge to do everything at once as much as you possibly can!

I could ask you, if you do, how often do you think about what happened to that small child who used to wish upon a star? Who wanted something so very badly and deep in your heart, and genuinely believed it could come true for you? Listening to fairytales about being rescued into happiness, you would feel the happy ending knowing it can be. You can – the present-day you can, too, as you find the realization that every moment of every day is another chance to use to get there, to where you want to go and how you want to feel slim, healthy and happy for life … Slim for Life.

You know how you want to feel and how you want to look. You know what you want your friends to say about you, where you want to go and what you want to wear. You know how to get there now and you can, too, as you remember that feeling … the pleasure of knowing that every moment is an opportunity to feel good about yourself. And you can do that now, with help from that little shining, sparkling star inside you that's granting your every wish to come true, for you.

Failure does not exist. Your degree of success only ever needs to be measured by you, yourself … and even your smallest degree of success is a seed for the future, and it will grow with any attention at all that you give it. Fear is always a fantasy, while success is always real and is tangible.

So, as you reflect on the learnings of today, you know what to do … Go ahead and give yourself an opportunity to carefully review and rehearse. Imagine every moment, experience every sound, and see it all clearly in your mind like watching yourself in your mind's own blockbuster movie. Let your subconscious mind go over and over it with you to review and practice it carefully, step by step. You can even rewind and play it back all the way through, or even stop the action here and there until you're completely clear on how you will do it. Go ahead now, review every part as often as you need to, and know it is a part of you - you are Slim for Life!

Let it feel good. Believe it. Don't waste my time or yours. Allow it to happen. Let that little star inside you dazzle because each and every suggestion you have ever heard me utter is registered deep within your subconscious mind.

You accept now, without the slightest reservation, the total responsibility for your body, your health, comfort, wellbeing, and happiness. You are now your own person - proud, confident and in control with that problem finally resolved.

And so before coming back from that place and returning to this place, I'd like you to take a moment to remember every positive thought you've ever had about yourself ... and smile ... How good does that feel?

Step #9: Gain Confidence

Relieve feelings of self-consciousness.

Improve self-confidence, body confidence and self-belief.

While listening to the hypnosis audio for Step #9 the deeply therapeutic, meditative process will enhance mental, emotional, physical and spiritual relaxation, promoting self-healing whether you're listening to the audio, or going about your daily business.

Slim for Life Step #9: Gain Confidence takes you through a process of self-recognition and release of any unwanted, no longer useful, self-limiting beliefs. It changes them to give you an even greater perspective and rationalization of difficult situations, both past and present, as you unlearn fear and lack of confidence.

Can you notice how easy it is to let go of all self-doubt, release worries about what others think, let go of self-consciousness and lack of self-esteem, replacing these with self-value and self-preservation? This is a most valuable part of this life-changing experience.

Here, lasting feelings of calm enable you to sense peaceful, self-assurance and an end to all kinds of self-defeating, sabotaging behaviour. Speaking to yourself kindly and in more nurturing tones, praising yourself for the decisions you're making through inner strength, with clarity and taking charge as you're dealing easily with everyday demands without feeling overwhelmed.

Developing an attitude and approach to life of gratitude and so grateful for your wonderful healthy body. New thought patterns lead to success, motivation and new possibilities. Feeling stronger with increased energy levels, improved health and greatly reduced stress. More body confidence as your vision of the slimmer you is taking shape right now and enjoying self-satisfaction, relief and self-belief that shows in your face and posture, and your vocal utterances, in what you wear and how you wear it.

Stepping into that new body - a brand new you who is feeling naturally at ease, naturally confident and relaxed with your surroundings regardless of whether anyone is watching or you are alone. It really is ALL about you.

Enjoy the hypnotic audio – and remember, for maximum effectiveness, listen daily for 7 days.

Praise yourself when you deserve it...
Be kind to yourself often...
Enjoy the new You!

READ-ALONG HYPNOSIS - STEP #9

The best way to benefit from the Slim for Life™ hypnosis experience is to upgrade to the full online program, which contains the audio tracks.

The following pages contain a version of the tracks converted into a "read-along" format, which will serve as a wonderful preview and jumpstart into what awaits you inside the full program.

~ ~ ~ ~ ~ ~ ~ ~

I recommend sitting comfortably and reading this hypnotic excerpt slowly, imagining that I'm speaking directly with you:

Take a moment to think again about how much weight you intend to release. Think about your target weight, your ideal size and perfect shape. Think about how good you will feel, how good you will look and how proud you can be achieving that slim, healthy body you deserve. Get that vision really clear in your mind.

Enjoy the feeling of allowing my words to register deep into the subconscious part of your mind as you become receptive to my suggestions which are entirely for your benefit and wellbeing.

Once again, allow a few deep breaths and relax yourself from head to toe. Imagine that you're breathing in peace and harmony, and with each easy outward breath I'd like you to release any stress or tension. That's right, breathe in self-confidence now and let go of all self-doubt.

Allow yourself to turn the world off while you while you focus on your own personal wellbeing. Be thankful for your goal of releasing all excess weight to feel absolutely great. Take a moment to recognize some of the changes you're already making. As one of my mentors Earl Nightingale said, "Success is the progressive realization of a worthy ideal." You're smoothly moving forward on this weight loss journey now, so embrace your progress ... on being Slim for Life.

Allow yourself to effortlessly release all self-doubt and connect with your inner wisdom. Release old hurts and feel a deep sense of love for yourself as well as those you care about. Decide to nurture, comfort, trust and empower yourself to become the very best version of yourself. Follow your path to freedom.

It is from positive experiences that you learn how to use your self-confidence in a way that builds and grows stronger every day. Enjoy increased feelings of self-worth as you recognize now more than ever before that only good and positive thoughts, feelings and emotions are of value to you. Negative thoughts damage you. You now allow only good and positive thoughts, feelings and emotions to influence your life experience.

It can be easy to be that person who does not allow for mistakes to be made, and so it can be quite comforting to know that an error is simply an opportunity to do things differently next time. Perfection is seldom needed. You may have noticed that even Olympic athletes are never perfect all the time and sometimes get things wrong, even when they win. Interestingly, the Cherokee Indians, when they weave their beautiful rugs and blankets, always leave a knot or a slight imperfection so that the gods are never angered or think that they are trying to be gods themselves. Of course, that's a story about what is really important and what is not.

You now look to the future, knowing it's ok if you leave a knot somewhere. Decide that things will go well, that you will succeed. You are special and important, attractive, capable, resourceful, and slim, healthy and happy. Program your mind to succeed at your goal. Look into your future and see only good things happening to you as you move forward to grasp opportunities, intensely aware that all your worthwhile goals are attainable. Whatever the mind can conceive and believe, it will achieve.

Congratulate yourself on your achievements in life. From this day forward you have all the self-confidence you need to build upon and all the capabilities and capacities to be that beautiful, slim person that you are ... Slim for Life. You now take control of your life and your emotions, trusting your judgement and trusting yourself to be ok. You are committed to your wellbeing and your goals, concentrating fully on what's important to you.

Others around you notice you and appreciate you more as you demonstrate your self-confidence. Your positive approach allows others to have confidence in you and as your confidence grows and manifests itself in your day-to-day successes, your creativity discovers new ways of expressing itself to become a powerfully effective part of your own special personality. You impress and amaze others with your clarity of thought and expression of new ideas. You now step into your own power, establishing yourself as that interesting, elegant, positive person that you are ... as you are being Slim for Life.

You can now recognize that you are the equal of all as you feel relaxed, calm, self-confident and comfortable in every situation, willing to embrace greater clarity as you unlearn that old feeling of fear and lack of confidence.

Take a deep breath now and relax yourself from head to toe while you take into your mind the image of you, Slim for Life. You feel happy, safe and secure, self-confident and self-assured, and loving your new body as you tell yourself 'I can ... I will ... I am ... Things will go well!' The regular practice of focusing on this picture of yourself with that wonderful 'feelgood' state is your natural way of being. It's all about you feeling good about you as you notice that all fear and all self-doubt leaves you completely.

You now unlearn fear by being positive and knowing that the only thing that can hurt you is the fear itself. No longer do you accept fear and negativity as you release and banish right now all unwanted inappropriate thoughts, symptoms, feelings and behaviours.

From this day forward you allow only good and positive thoughts, feelings and emotions to grow within you, becoming an integral part of your own perfect personality. You do this easily because you are taking control of your thoughts, your life, your body and your emotions.

Now hold that image of the new you. Allow wonderful feelings to be something that expand. See that beautiful feeling now as a pulsating white light, warm and comfortable, powerful, empowering ... and allow that white light to expand and grow so that it encompasses you. You are completely contained within a brilliant protective cocoon of pulsating white light. Enjoy that warm and comfortable feeling, and confident and admiring thoughts about you and your special qualities and capacities, as it fills you from the top of your head now, down through to the tips of your fingers and the tips of your toes. Feel that wonderful feeling growing and expanding as it fills your entire being with its power and positive influence.

Allow that white light to be absorbed into your body completely and permanently to your highest benefit, along with all of those good and positive feelings you've ever had about yourself. From this moment forward, you are the confident. self-assured person that you want to be, that you deserve to be, that you are right now.

Each and everything you do, you now do better than you have ever done before; completely at ease in a completely relaxed frame of mind and knowing that you are calm, relaxed and self-confident. You are proud to be you!

Accepting now, without the slightest reservation, the total responsibility for your body, your health, comfort, wellbeing, happiness and self-confidence. You are now your own person - proud, confident and in control with that problem finally resolved.

And so before coming back from that place and returning to this place, I'd like you to take a moment to remember every positive thought you've ever had about yourself ... and smile ... How good does that feel?

Step #10: Enjoy Food!

Stop criticizing yourself.

Stop worrying about what other people think.

Simply enjoy your mind/body makeover and new, healthy lifestyle more than you ever thought possible.

You can eat what you want and still release excess weight!

While listening to the hypnosis audio for Step #10 you'll experience a deeply therapeutic meditative process that is again life-changing. A feeling of whole mind and body relaxation from the top of your head and down to the tips of your fingers and tips of your toes that will stay with you long after you complete the Slim for Life series.

Slim for Life Step #10: Enjoy Food! enables subconscious reinforcement of Steps #1 through to #9 of this mind and body makeover and further tuning in the taste buds to enjoy only what's good for you.

You'll experience a sense of upgraded self-awareness with recognition that because you are eating everything in smaller portions, you can eat exactly what you fancy. Enjoying, aromas, colours, tastes and textures of foods instead of counting calories, measuring your progress thus far and allowing a deep-rooted sense of satisfaction and pride at taking control of your weight, instead of it controlling you.

Feelings of perfect inner peace and security continue to promote self-healing as you no longer entertain ideas of self-criticism or worrying what other people think. Very much decreased mind chatter allows you to think only the thoughts you want to think about yourself, taking control of your life, your habits, feelings and emotions to give you a sense of protection and being shielded from others' stress and negativity.

Sensing energy levels rising, improved health and vitality, no longer a sluggish, couch potato, and with regular, nourishing sleep patterns, feeling relaxed about just about everything as enormous portions of self-confidence and self-belief are at the forefront of your personality.

Continuing your journey of self-discovery and developing more and more the habits and behaviours of naturally slim. You're enjoying your mind and body makeover and new healthier, happier lifestyle more than you ever thought possible, and with that wonderful, incredible feeling of emotional freedom, joy and unconditional love for yourself and those you care about - all through recognizing that you really can eat what you want and still release ALL excess weight! You can enjoy food - you are Slim for Life!

Enjoy the hypnotic audio - and remember, for maximum effectiveness, listen daily for 7 days.

Change your thoughts and you literally change your life...

Happiness is simple. It's just being who you are - not pretending to be interesting, beautiful, funny or having to hang out with the in-crowd.

READ-ALONG HYPNOSIS – STEP #10

The best way to benefit from the Slim for Life™ hypnosis experience is to upgrade to the full online program, which contains the audio tracks.

The following pages contain a version of the tracks converted into a "read-along" format, which will serve as a wonderful preview and jumpstart into what awaits you inside the full program.

~ ~ ~ ~ ~ ~ ~ ~

I recommend sitting comfortably and reading this hypnotic excerpt slowly, imagining that I'm speaking directly with you:

Take a moment to think again about how much weight you intend to release. Think about your target weight, your ideal size and perfect shape. Think about how good you will feel, how good you will look and how proud you can be achieving that slim, healthy body you deserve. Get that vision really clear in your mind.

Enjoy the feeling of allowing my words to register deep into the subconscious part of your mind as you become receptive to my suggestions which are entirely for your benefit and wellbeing.

I'd like you to take a few deeper breaths now, imaging that you're breathing in self-love and self-congratulations, and with each easy outward breath, releasing anything and everything that may have been holding you back from achieving the slim, healthy, happy body you desire. Focus easily and constantly on your personal wellbeing and weight release journey. How good does it feel for you?

I'd like to congratulate you on the decision that you have made, to take on for yourself fully, the responsibility for your own life - and to respect and protect your own body. It is with our body that we enjoy all the good things of life and you decided it's time to take the action you need to take, to change those ways of doing things in that way, to the right way for you.

Memory and taste are distinctly woven in the mind, giving each of us our own range of tasty remembering. We can pause and wonder about the tastes that excite us, those that intrigue and enthral us. Many are reminders from childhood - like Grandma's home-baked cakes and fish and chips every Friday, and Mum's deliciously tasty Sunday roasted lamb with mint sauce, or beef with Yorkshire puddings served with dark red cabbage, bright orange carrots, roasting crispy potatoes; all with plenty of greens and of course smothered with delicious gravy. Always a desert for afterwards like treacle pudding and custard. Home-made all sorts, like toast and jam.

Ooh, and all the yummy sweets from childhood like

seaside rock, hard candy shaped like pieces of ribbon tasting of aniseed, peanutty crunch, banana splits, circles of raspberry and strawberry and many bright colours of joy. None of which tastes the way we imagine today which can also be said of Christmas too. Take a yellow sweet and unwrap the cellophane, it's certain to be lemon but tastes of liquorice instead and green lime of cinnamon with soft centres - and cherry reds tasting of vanilla or ginger combined with almost indecipherable sweetness of honey or cloves and lemons. Ahh, the many and varied tastes of childhood that are our mysterious and timely reminders of home.

Holiday flavours too can juggle in the mind like those pungent garlicky dips with freshly caught fish and adorable salads of rich red tomatoes, yellow and green peppers, salty anchovy and olives in blacks and greens. Juicy tropical orange and pineapple or an icy glass of lemonade while listening to the sounds of the waves. Ice creams all creamy and smooth as they melt irresistibly on the tongue. The sweet and sour of it all tastes delicious.

Some consider chocolate is an emotional food, lingering like love long after the first heady taste has disappeared. History teaches us that more than 3,000 years ago, cocoa plants were first cultivated in Mesoamerica by the Olmec tribe living in southern Mexico. Legendary Aztec leader Montezuma was known to drink whole goblets of rich hot chocolate every day to enhance his display of power, ardour and opulence before his evening of indulgence in his harem.

A holy feast of breaking bread and drinking wine ... Food for redemption, feasts for freedom, and all sorts of commemorations remind us that whole fortunes of nations have been built on the desire for spice alone as ships sailed the rough seas of this beautiful world in search of new tastes and new experiences to share. The simple pleasures of taste and smell filling us with contentment and joy, evoking new delights just like those Christmas candies that soothe and delight. Evocative tastes lingering in the mind with pleasant comfort and effortless joy.

Let us not forget to wake up and smell the coffee!

Sometimes the effect of years passing and the natural bodily changes that have been happening to you and perhaps even recent events in your life have in various ways caused you to not be as slim as you wished to be. Your subconscious mind is in charge of everything going on inside the body, including each organ, cell and nerve. Your subconscious mind can work consciously and constantly to ensure that a permanently slim, healthy body is achievable and easily sustainable - ensuring that awareness of hunger is accurate and that only a small portion of healthy, nutritious food is eaten ... chewing slowly and thoroughly and enjoyed more than ever before. Immediately before the feeling of satiation you will stop eating completely. You can re-programme the mind to develop a new body image of a slimmer, happier, healthier person practising that visualization and changing the daily instructions in behaviour so that eating really does become so very unimportant while the urge to become slim, healthy and happy takes priority.

When you began this Slim for Life journey of ten steps to permanent weight release, you had a dream in mind; something important that you wanted to make happen. 'I would if I could' has a new meaning now because the words that go through your mind many times a day comfortably are 'I can ... I will ... I am' ... Deep in your heart, you truly believe this and begin to feel the pride and the self-confidence that makes it all happen for you, for life.

You feel comfortable with your past, recognizing that your past provides many valuable experiences and learnings for you. So as you relax and let your mind go with this flow, you refuse to live your life with any form of negativity or guilt, especially guilt around food. What you did in the past was the best you could do at the time. You are better now, more relaxed and more in control now seeing yesterday through today's eyes. You have matured and grown and you understand that there is no value in negativity. Only learning and experience have value for you.

Your childhood programming and experiences were formed by circumstantial accidents so keep the pieces you like and agree with, but any thoughts, feelings, habits, emotions ... any depressive thought patterns, doubts or fears that might live inside you ... can all be released with immediate effect.

Each day happens your way as you take control of your eating habits, and you honestly believe that you now have all the resources you need to succeed, noticing this feeling increasingly every day. Relax and embrace that attitude, for what you are doing right now is choosing to turn the world off to relax and feel a sense of control greater than you have ever had. That is your reality. Keep it and use it.

So go ahead now and review every part in your mind. Go over it as often as you need to ... to know it is a part of you. It's all about you. It is you - you are Slim for Life.

You accept now, without the slightest reservation, the total responsibility for your body, your health, comfort, wellbeing, and happiness.

You are now your own person - proud, confident and in control with that problem finally resolved.

And so before coming back from that place and returning to this place, I'd like you to take a moment to remember every positive thought you've ever had about yourself ... and smile ... Congratulations! How good does that feel?

Claire Willmott

Morning all, I just wanted to share that a week in and the scales are going down already but I don't feel deprived of anything at all!
I thought I was going to be really daunted but the trickiest thing is actually trying to find the time for myself each day to listen to the recording... moral of the story - sometimes it's ok to put yourself first, and when you realise that you'll be amazed at the positive impact on your life!
After only one week I'm already feeling a huge impact so I'm excited to see what the rest of my life brings!

Tina Heath and 8 others — 11 Comments

Jayne Stanley
I've just completed week one. Great changes already, feeling so much better and confident that this is working.x

Like Reply 1w

Sarah Jane

I wanted to post my successes on here as I am so pleased with how things are happening on the Slim For Life Plan with Tina Heath.
Physically, my body aches less and I have learnt that is due to me being so much more relaxed due to the hypnotherapy sessions 😊
My waist is getting smaller 😊. I don't want to weigh myself but I know my body is releasing my body fat by how I feel. 😊
Mentally, I am feeling calm and balanced. I no longer crave food as my calming or numbing strategy. In fact I have been utterly amazed how small my meals have become and feeling very satisfied 😊
I am trusting the plan and letting my body choose my meals. 😊
My shopping and costs have nearly halved as I used to be a binge eater 😊
The plan has given me the gift of going deep enough into my subconscious mind to find a way of healing. It has been the one piece of the puzzle that was missing for 35 years. I recently realised how diets were so toxic to my mental health but I could not get well on my own and stop my disordered eating 😊
I am now optimistic and looking forwards to being a size 14. I am a size 22 at the moment and I absolutely know I will be a size 14 by my next birthday. 😊
Thank you Tina 🌸

Tina Heath and 11 others — 7 Comments

Sian Lloyd

Hi
Well I am totally amazed! I am taking the plan slowly so my subconscious has time to let the advice sink in.

Yesterday after a pretty stressful day- I was able to walk past the confectionery aisle and say no to myself.

I am losing inches- some weight- but as it's taken me 40+ years to get to my current size- I am taking the route of the tortoise- slowly and one step at a time.

I am a recovering chocoholic and my name is Sian I absolutely love your programme- you are retraining me so well.

Thank you so much x it is so much appreciated after so many negative years of subconsciously sabotaging many mainstream diets as I have been unable a accept success at very personal level.

At Slim for Life I am the one in control not the calories or of other people or their opinions. I cannot say enough praise for the program. I am still human, but instead of eating everything delicious and calorific, I will only buy one treat instead of buying the whole store.

You, Tina Heath and 6 others — 7 Comments

Take Stock of Your Success:

Be Realistic

Write down 10 changes you've noticed.

For example, enjoying smaller portions, fewer crisps, stopped snacking and picking between meals, less chocolate, fewer sweets, fewer biscuits, no sugar in cups of tea/coffee, less alcohol, fewer desserts, etc.

1.____

2.____

3.____

4.____

5.____

6.____

7.____

8.____

9.____

10._______________________________________

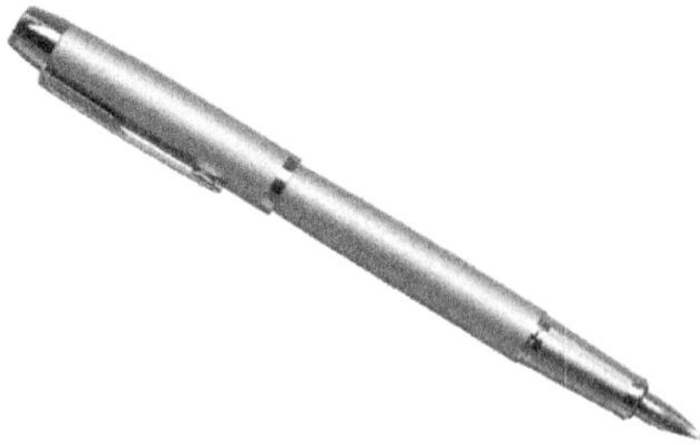

Make a note of 10 things you used to think you liked eating and drinking but now realize you no longer like the taste of.

For example, sugar, dairy products, crisps, nuts, fizzy drinks and sodas.

1.____

2.____

3.____

4.____

5.____

6.____

7.____

8.____

9.____

10._______________________________________

What have you learned about yourself through this program?

How do you feel about your progress?

When you feel slim,
you feel happy and
you keep feeling happy...

Then only happy people,
circumstances and
situations can come
into your life.

Practice feeling
as you wish to be...

Don't forget your
Goal Card –
it's vital to help to
keep you on track.

About The Author

Dr. Tina Heath is a transpersonal psychologist with more than 30 years of experience studying and working with human behaviour, incorporating hypnotherapy, Neurolinguistics, Meta-Medicine diagnostic techniques, emotional healing and regression therapy.

Passionate about human potential, Tina is completely driven to help people find the emotional freedom to live the life they deserve.

Slim for Life is the culmination of around 30 years of research and development, trial and experience of helping people just like you to release excess weight through personal consultations, group classes and special events.

We thank you for your interest in this program and wish you every possible success in your weight-release journey.

We will be delighted to hear your personal success story, together with before and after pictures when you feel brave enough to share!

Please send them to: **support@slimforlife.co.uk**

Remember, we are here for you, every step of your journey to Slim for Life! **Have fun!**

ILFORD
HP5 PLUS
tinaheathuk
Liked by healthcareforyourmind and 13 others
tinaheathuk My Passion - Recording Hypnotherapy
@healthcareforyourmind #hypnosis
#hypnotherapist #hypnotherapy... more
tinaheathuk
Hayling Island Beach
Liked by healthcareforyourmind and 16 others
tinaheathuk Early morning walkies #sandisland
#lowtide @jessheath_1 @harrietbluebelle
@bill.rowlands @healthcareforyourmind... more
tinaheathuk
Liked by healthcareforyourmind and 14 others
tinaheathuk Unleash the Power Within
#firewalker #upw #tonyrobbins #newyork
@tonyrobbins @healthcareforyourmind
@travelyourownpath @beautifulsoulsnonprofit

About The Music

Inside the full Slim for Life program, each hypnosis track is supported by music that touches your body, mind and soul!

Creative music enhances the mood and helps to deepen the meditative experience enabling the conscious, subconscious and higher conscious energies to become more easily aligned, and the subliminal suggestions to take effect more quickly, easily to become a permanent part of your personality.

Samhain Carter-Brazier, Composer and Producer at Mayfield Studios, at Portsmouth, Hampshire, UK – has created some unique music for a diverse range of projects and has a wealth of knowledge and experience when it comes to tailor-making music for a project such as this. His ability, coupled with the knowhow of Tina, has contributed greatly to the field of health and wellbeing over the years.

The music for Slim for Life has been specifically written to support, enhance and deepen the hypnotic experience, assisting the subconscious mind in adapting to these ideas, creating a full mind/body relaxation which culminates in a feeling of long-lasting inner peace.

We've incorporated some tones from the ancient "Solfeggio frequencies," believed to enable spiritual blessings, healing and transformation when played or sung in harmony, providing the brain with new stimuli to help in keeping it young, healthy and active.

The Solfeggio Frequencies, a vocal note scale (do, re, mi, fa, so, la, ti, do) is adapted from an invention by an 11th century monk named Guido D'Arezzo. The tones we've used here help you to feel happier, more relaxed and less anxious, creating positive shifts in our thinking, especially when listened to regularly.

UT - 396 Hz - Liberating Guilt and Fear - this frequency has awakening qualities. It cleans and releases feelings of guilt and grief, the basic obstacles to success in any aspect of life, turning them into joy. It eradicates fear, deep within the subconscious part of the mind and gives power to your dreams and goals.

RE - 417 Hz - Undoing Situations and Facilitating Change - Liberating negative thought and behavioural patterns from deep within the subconscious part of the mind and releasing past trauma, and negative energy from the body to embrace change and new beginnings.

MI - 528 Hz - Transformation and Miracles (DNA Repair) - known as the Love Frequency, Miracle Tone and Frequency of Transformation due to its powerful effects on the human body in terms of reducing cortisol and releasing stress as it revitalizes energy. It boosts confidence, body confidence and self-esteem.

FA - 639 Hz - Connecting/Relationships. This frequency encourages cell repair within the physical body. It enables us to connect and balance harmonious interpersonal relationships - here used, to strengthen our relationship with ourselves. It boosts communication, understanding and tolerance, social confidence and love.

SOL - 741 Hz - Awakening Intuition - used for solving problems, and awakening the mind's own healing powers. It cleans the cells from a variety of electromagnetic radiations, detoxifying the cells and organs to improve health, happiness, stability and appreciation of life. Purification of mind and body enabling us to find the solutions we're seeking and express ourselves more fully.

LA - 852 Hz - Returning to Spiritual Order - this frequency raises our awareness and returns us to spiritual order - the Divinity we received at birth. It improves communication, awakens our knowledge about ourselves, enabling us to use our intuition more wisely.

TI - 963 Hz - Awakening the Pineal Gland - whole mind-body healing, raising our vibrations into cellular alignment and reconnecting us with life, love and the rest of the world. Returning us to Oneness, of positive energy and reconnecting us with our Source.

To explore the work of **Samhain Carter-Brazier** and dive deeper into the magical world of meditation in music, go to: https://carterbrazier.com

The Spiritual Viewpoint

> Everything is first worked out in the unseen before it is manifested in the seen, in the ideal before it is realized in the real, in the spiritual before it shows forth in the material. The realm of the unseen is the realm of cause. The realm of the seen is the realm of effect. The unseen or the invisible cannot be detected by our senses, but that doesn't mean it does not exist. The invisible or the unseen is where all creation comes from. Your thoughts are invisible. Your feelings are invisible. Your beliefs are invisible. To understand how all creation comes from the invisible, take a look at anything created by a human being and you will find without exception that it began in the invisible - with a thought. Thoughts are cause and our material world is the effect.

~ Ralph Waldo Trine, 1897

Upgrade Your Experience

By Joining The Full Slim for Life™ Program!

Sit back, *relax*...
From now on,
you don't have to
do a thing.
(Try it for
yourself!)

~ Dr. Tina Heath

- ✓ Results Guaranteed When You Follow The Program!
- ✓ Instant Access To The Entire Program Online
- ✓ All 10 Slim for Life™ Hypnosis MP3 Audios
- ✓ The Slim for Life™ Guidebook PDF
- ✓ **BONUS:** Weight Release Goal Card
- ✓ **BONUS:** Slim for Life™ **Pedometer**
- ✓ **BONUS:** "Notes To Self" **Affirmation Card Deck**
- ✓ **BONUS:** Clarity of Thought Hypnosis MP3 Audio
- ✓ **BONUS:** Release Depression Hypnosis MP3 Audio
- ✓ **BONUS:** Embrace Your Style Hypnosis MP3 Audio
- ✓ **BONUS:** Sleep Well Hypnosis MP3 Audio

Order Now | Get Instant Access!

www.SlimforLife.co.uk

Watch The FREE Quick Start Video!

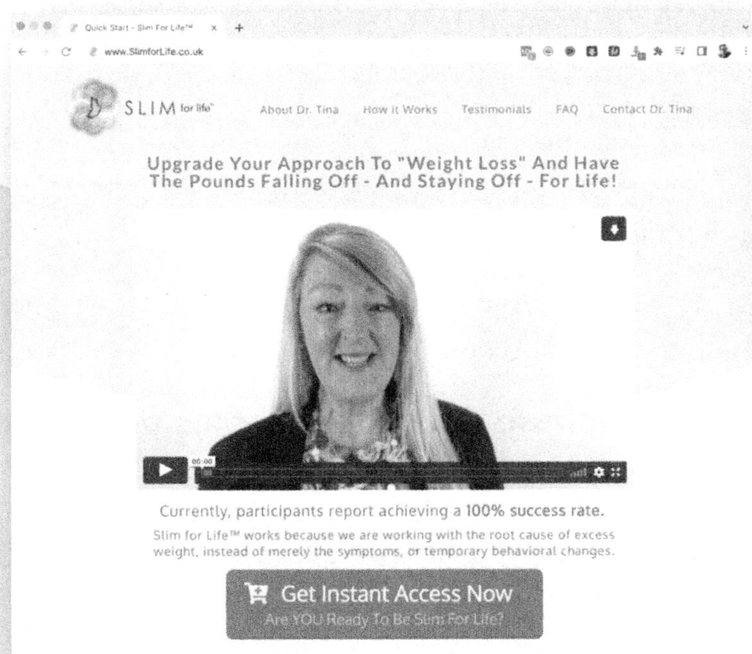

Getting Started Is Easy…

www.SlimforLife.co.uk

Love This Book?

Please share the transformation and possibility with your friends and family!

We are on a mission to increase the world's level of awareness about what it really takes to be slim, happy, and healthy - for life.

You can play an important role in your own community and inner circle.

Please consider buying copies of this book for the people in your life whom you know are ready for positive change.

You can purchase additional copies and direct others here:

https://www.SlimforLife.co.uk/book

SLIM
FOR
LIFE
10 Easy Steps
To Permanent Weight Loss
Through Hypnotherapy
Dr. Tina Heath

Printed in Great Britain
by Amazon

28669072R00104